The North Prospect
of Winsor Castle By
M. Knife—

To Susan.

I hope you will one day visit this historic castle

Kathie Whelan.

(front end paper) Bird's eye view of Windsor Castle.

(back end paper) The Royal Lodgings in the time of Charles II. King's Lodgings are shown blue, Queen's Lodgings red, and the colour coding darkens as the rooms grow harder of access.

i (previous page) Disused heads for supporting the helms of the Garter Knights on the canopys of the choir stalls, now in the undercroft of the Curfew Tower.

ii (facing page) Queen Victoria and Prince Albert going out through the George IV Gate. From Nash's *Windsor Castle*.

WINDSOR

THE MOST ROMANTIC CASTLE

Mark Girouard

Hodder & Stoughton

LONDON SYDNEY AUCKLAND

TO ELIZABETH MANNERS

British Library Cataloguing in Publication Data

Girouard, Mark
  Windsor: The Most Romantic Castle
  I. Title
  942. 296

  ISBN 0 - 340 - 59504 - 3
  Copyright © Mark Girouard 1993

  First published in Great Britain 1993

Published by Hodder and Stoughton, a division of Hodder and Stoughton Ltd, Mill Road, Dunton Green, Sevenoaks, Kent TN13 2YA
Editorial Office: 47 Bedford Square, London WC1B 3DP

Book design by Dorothy Girouard

Printed in Great Britain by Butler & Tanner Ltd, Frome & London

WINDSOR THE MOST ROMANTIC CASTLE

Mark Girouard

ACKNOWLEDGEMENTS

I must acknowledge the gracious permission of Her Majesty the Queen to make use of material in the Royal Archives. I am most grateful for the prompt and knowledgeable help I have received from members of the Queen's Household, especially from Geoffrey de Bellaigue and Christopher Lloyd in the Royal Collection, Jane Roberts in the Royal Library, Sheila de Bellaigue and Frances Dimond in the Royal Archives, and Gwyneth Campling, Picture Manager at Windsor Castle. I must also thank Roland Wiseman, Deputy Ranger of Windsor Great Park, for information and for help over photography.

The Dean of Windsor and Mrs Mitchell, the staff of St George's Chapel and Dr Eileen Scarff, Archivist to the Chapter, made working on the Lower Ward a pleasure. I must thank Richard Hewlings, and David Batchelor of English Heritage for an illuminating tour of the fire-damaged portion of the Castle and of the Round Tower, Sophie Andreae, Geoffrey Parnell and John Thorneycroft for information and help over drawings, and Stephen Croad, of the National Monuments Record, for expediting photographs. The section on St George's Hall was the brain-child of my wife, and made possible through the creative assistance of Rickie Burdett, Sarah Hopkins, Sian Harcourt and Philippa Thomas of the Architecture Foundation, with help from Giles Worsley of *Country Life* over background material. I have enjoyed working with Richard Cohen, who first asked me to write the book, my editor, Delian Bower, Jamie Hodder-Williams and Jane Lawson at Hodder and Stoughton, and Anne-Marie Ehrlich, ever-resourceful purveyor of illustrations. Mike Shaw, Marion Cookson and Sophie Janson at Curtis Brown never failed to soothe and help me. As with previous books, Harland Walshaw and Peter Burton took endless trouble over photography, and Elizabeth Manners's contribution was invaluable, not least her compilation of the index, with the help of my daughter Blanche.

1 (right)Windsor Castle from the air.

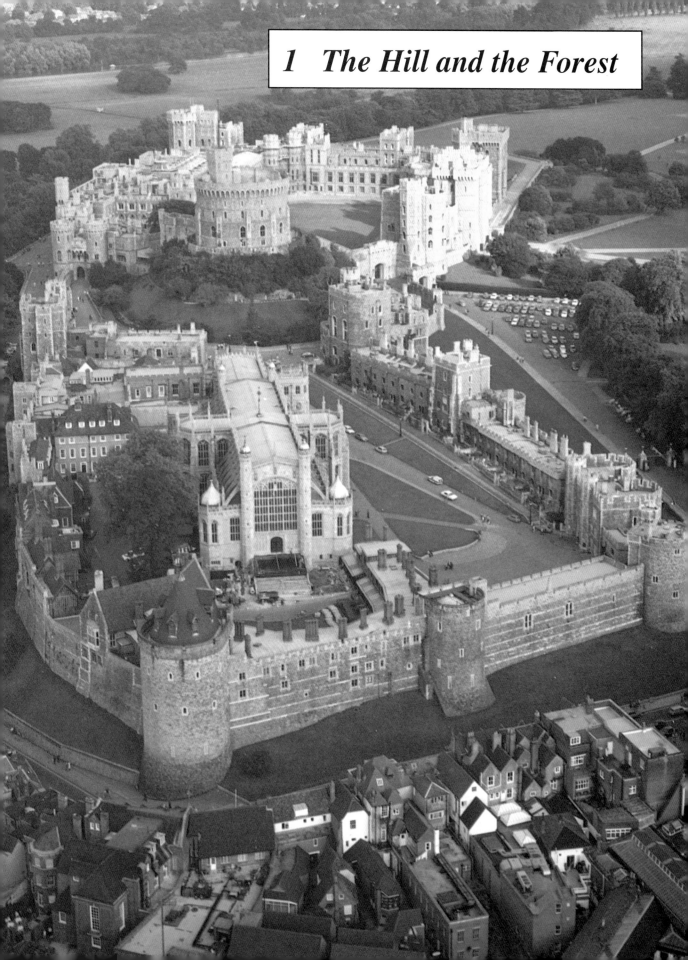

Windsor Castle grew out of a hill and a forest. The forest was one in the old sense of the word, a huge area of wild country, mixed heath and woodland, where deer and wild boar roamed. The Saxon kings who came to hunt in it built a house down by the Thames at a village called Windsor, and named the forest after it. When Edward the Confessor died he left house and forest to Westminster Abbey. William the Conqueror bought them back. According to a charter of the time "that place seemed suitable and convenient by reason of the nearness of the water and a forest fit for the chase and diverse other things therein that are proper for Kings".

About two miles away from the Saxon palace was a chalk bluff, rising gently from the south and dropping down a steep one hundred feet to the Thames. There is some evidence that it had been occupied in Iron Age and Roman times, but it seems to have been uninhabited since then. A hill by a river was an obvious site for a castle, and William I built one there. It followed the usual form of Norman castles: a keep on an artificial mound, and fortified enclosures or wards to either side of it. Henry I moved his court from the Saxon palace to the new castle, and the name followed it. The Saxon village became Old Windsor, and a new Windsor town grew up below the castle.

William the Conqueror's castle was built of wood. Between the mid-twelfth and mid-thirteenth centuries Henry II and Henry III turned the wooden castle into a stone one. Henry II re-built the round tower on its mound, and constructed a stone wall round the Upper Ward, punctuated by square towers. Henry III made a similar conversion to the Lower Ward, but square towers had gone out of fashion for fortifications, and his were rounded (Pl. 3). By Henry III's reign, or soon after, two parks had been enclosed within the forest, for safe-keeping of the deer. By his death in 1272, in fact, the shape of Windsor had been fixed: a castle on a hill, a round tower on a mound, two wards with walls and towers round them, all for power and prestige; and to the south of the hill two parks, one large and one small, for pleasure. For the next seven hundred years all that was to be done was to fill and re-fill this outline.

The result is extraordinary. Most people must have had the experience of seeing Windsor Castle unexpectedly. They may be driving on the motorway, or walking in the Great Park, talking or thinking of other things; they shift their line of vision for some reason, and there it is. The experience is a little like coming across a big ship in a town on an inland waterway; suddenly there is this huge object, rising above the houses, and different from them.

The metaphor of a ship is relevant, for like a ship Windsor Castle is not just an object but a container for large numbers of people —six hundred or more in the most populated periods of its history, royal class in the bows, religious class in the stern, and over and below and around the passengers the servants and crew that look after the ship and make the passengers comfortable.

To discover how all these people were organised and how they interacted with each other over the centuries can be enjoyable and intriguing. One could call it a kind of industrial archaeology, except that so often one does not have to dig: Yeomen of the Ewery and Pantry, Pages of the Backstairs, Military Knights, Keepers of the Privy Purse and others are still there in action.

But as with a ship, one ends up asking oneself where the whole organisation is going, and how, and why. One can see Windsor as the expression of a constant battle to maintain and if possible increase power. It started as a seat of power in the most straightforward way, a fortified place with a garrison in it. Edward III's founding of the Order of the Garter was not just the putting of a group of people into fancy dress but a way of bolstering and supporting his power, by binding them to him with ties of gratitude and loyalty and strengthening the relationship with ceremony and religion. The Lower Ward at Windsor, with St George's Chapel at its heart, was transformed as a result, and the beauty and splendour that emerged fostered the image, and therefore the power, of the monarch.

In the Upper Ward a different kind of image-boosting was going on, as the monarch lived with the appropriate degree of magnificence in an appropriately magnificent setting. What was considered appropriate varied with the centuries, however, and royal life changed, and the buildings with it. By the 1680s the medieval St George's Hall was unacceptably old-fashioned; as the monarch could not afford to seem out of date it was accordingly transformed, and Verrio brought in to use new baroque techniques of apotheosis, and launch Charles II on clouds of glory in its ceiling. One hundred and forty years later it was transformed again. Medieval and castle images were relevant once more, as symbols of tradition in a society threatened by revolution. The hall was re-medievalised, and most of the castle with it.

In 1824, when justifying the spending of large sums of public money on this re-modelling, the Chancellor of the Exchequer talked of the "degree of splendour that was becoming the sovereign who ruled over the country, but also the country over which he ruled". The suitability of splendour was an old concept, but he was also suggesting something new. One function of the Castle, and the monarch in it, was now to express the power and prosperity of the nation. As a result, at both Windsor Castle and Buckingham Palace, one finds an odd development: palaces growing grander as their occupants grow less powerful.

The monarchy survived because it accepted the situation, even if at first unwillingly, adapted to it and used its own mystique to support a new role. As well as the concept of standing for the greatness of the nation this role involved its Bagehotian rights to be consulted, to encourage and to warn, and the concept that it should stand for nationally accepted ideals, most obviously the ideal of family life. One can see the result at Windsor: State Visits at one end of the Upper Ward, Queen Victoria at her desk or in her Audience Chamber

2 (following page) The bird's-eye view of Windsor Castle drawn by Wenceslaus Hollar for Ashmole *Order of the Garter* (1672).

9

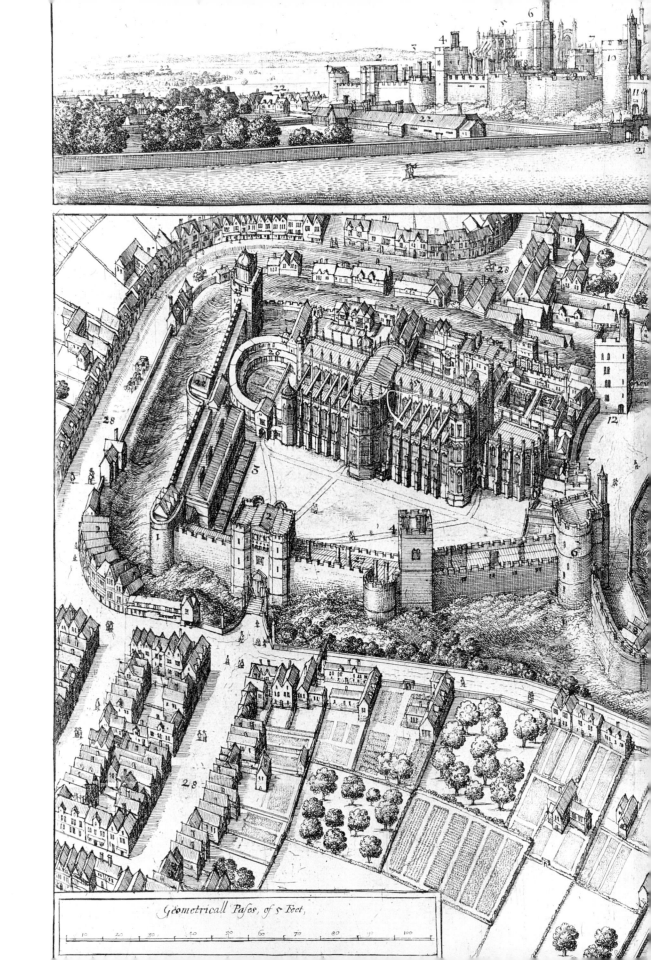

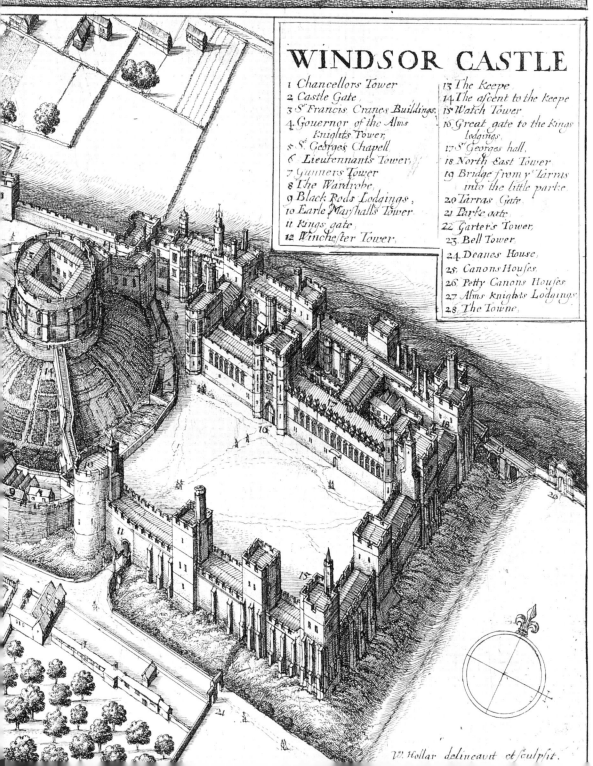

WINDSOR CASTLE

1 Chancellors Tower
2 Castle Gate
3 St Francis Cranes Buildings
4 Gouernor of the Alms Knights Tower
5 St Georges Chapell
6 Lieutennants Tower
7 Gunners Tower
8 The Wardrobe
9 Black Rods Lodgings
10 Earle Marshalls Tower
11 Kings gate
12 Winchester Tower

13 The Keepe
14 The ascent to the keepe
15 Watch Tower
16 Great gate to the Kings Lodgings
17 St Georges hall
18 North East Tower
19 Bridge from ye Tarras into the little parke
20 Tarras Gate
21 Parke gate
22 Garter's Tower
23 Bell Tower

24 Deanes House
25 Canons Houses
26 Petty Canons Houses
27 Alms knights Lodgings
28 The Towne

W. Hollar delineavit et sculpsit.

3 (above) The mid-fourteenth century Garter and Curfew Towers at the west end of the Lower Ward, seen from the town.

4 (right) Windsor Castle in the time of Queen Elizabeth. From the drawing by Hoefnagel.

encouraging and warning, and family life being lived in the Private Apartments, or in the privacy accepted as the family's due in the East Garden and Home Park.

No-one thought that the Queen was an ordinary wife and mother, however, least of all Queen Victoria herself. Her Assistant Private Secretary, Frederick Ponsonby, wrote of her that "she firmly believed that not only Kings and Queens, but even Princes, were on a higher plane than the rest of the human race". What gave, and still gives, Windsor Castle its especial vibrancy is the existence at its centre of a king or queen who know that they are different from other people, and are accepted as different by others. This belief derives from a variety of sources: their coronation, which sets the king or queen apart as the Lord's anointed; the long line of ancestors of which they are the culmination; perhaps something sacred which goes back beyond Christianity. It can give monarchs an aura and dignity in any situation; but to be effective they need other people who believe in their uniqueness as much as they do.

But kings and queens are also human beings. As human beings they have to come to terms with their kingship; some exploit it, some try to escape from it, some accept it and with it the duty to use it for good; some manage to combine the dignity of a monarch with human directness and warmth. It is interesting, and at times impressive, to watch kingship in action at Windsor; but the most poignant moments in its history come when one can watch monarchs as vulnerable human beings, subject to love, disease or death like everybody else: Richard II, in the Deanery before his last journey, lifting up his child wife to kiss her, putting her down, kissing her again, saying "goodbye my love, till we meet again," while the chronicler comments: "great pity was it that they separated, for they never saw each other more"; the sad, barely attended burial of Charles I, the black velvet pall turning white with the falling snow as it is carried down from the Upper Ward to St George's Chapel, the refusal of the commander of the garrison to allow a funeral service, and the coffin lowered into its vault "in silence and sorrow"; Lord Sydney, as a boy at Eton under George III, being taken by his aunt, the Lady Housekeeper at the Castle, to listen at the mad King's door: "if he were having a disturbed day he would be pacing up and down, and sometimes roaring; at other times the stillness would be broken by snatches of Handel as he groped in his darkness upon the keys of the harpsichord".

5 (right) Queen Elizabeth the Queen Mother, the present Queen, and Princess Margaret in the East Garden at Windsor, July 1941.

6 (far right) Henry VIII and his Garter Knights, and the Knights in Procession, from an illumination in the *Black Book of the Garter*. The heraldic mantles of the Knights are probably an invention of the illuminator.

The human problems of monarchy, its need to adapt to changing circumstances if it is to survive, its need for a constituency which can believe in it, are as critical today as they have ever been.

On 26 February, 1666, Samuel Pepys and his wife were taken on a tour of Windsor Castle by the organist and choir-master of St George's Chapel. They found the Chapel "a noble place indeed", and attended a service there, sitting on cushions specially brought for them among the stalls and banners of the Knights of the Garter. They listened to an anthem sung in their honour by the choirboys, and were impressed by the deep bowings towards the altar of the "Poor Knights", the retired military men who lived across the Lower Ward from the Chapel. They were taken to see the robes of the Garter Knights, and the chapel plate — magnificent enough, even though the jewel-studded reliquary that held the heart of St George, the silver and gold statue of St George himself on horseback, and many other treasures had been destroyed or sold at the Reformation. They saw the burial place of Henry VIII and Charles I, then went up to tour the Upper Ward and the Royal Lodgings, and marvel at the view from the terrace. Pepys summed it all up in his diary: "It is the most romantique castle that is in the world."

Its romance came partly from its hill-top position, partly from its royal associations, but also from the fact that, as the seat of the Order of the Garter, it was redolent of the age of chivalry and of the legendary age of King Arthur and his knights. The Chapel, with its rows of banners and helms above the stalls of the Knights, was the chapel of the Garter, not of the King; the Poor Knights, the choirboys, the canons and priests of the chapel were all adjuncts of the Order; and the main function of St George's Hall, in the Royal Lodgings, was to accommodate the Garter Feasts which at intervals filled the castle with colour, people and pageantry. For the Garter was famous all over Europe; as Selden put it, it "exceeds in majesty, honour and fame all Chivalrous Orders in the world".

In 1344 Edward III held a tournament at Windsor. It was a successful and brilliant occasion, and the evening after it was over the King made a dramatic oath before the assembled knights, laying his hand on the gospels as he did so. He was going to found a Round Table like that which King Arthur had founded at Camelot. It would consist of three hundred knights. Almost immediately his masons and carpenters set to work to construct a round building at Windsor to contain his Table. It was 200 feet in diameter, about four times the size of the Round Tower.

It was never finished, and has disappeared without trace. In 1346 Edward, claiming the kingdom of France as his by right, set sail for France, and fought the campaign of which the Battle of Crécy was to be the most famous episode. He was back by the end of 1347; and in 1348 he inaugurated a rather different Order of knighthood at Windsor. The knights had shrunk to the smaller, but more prestigious, number of twenty-six, including the King. Their patron saint was St George, their motto *Honi soit que mal y pense*. They acquired a prelate, a chancellor and a herald, were invested with their insignia by the King and installed at a religious ceremony in their Chapel. They were not called Knights of the Round Table but Knights of the Garter.

Why the garter? Why St George? Why the French motto? The founding of the Garter was to have momentous consequences for Windsor, but much about it remains obscure. The well-known story of the Countess of Salisbury dropping her garter is almost certainly apocryphal. The most convincing theory is that the Order grew out of Edward III's French campaign. The French motto, the literal translation of which is "Be he disgraced who thinks ill of it", could have been aimed at those who disputed Edward III's claim to France. The dark blue of the mantle was the colour of the royal French coat of arms. The name of St George was used as a battle cry by English troops on the French campaign: his adoption as patron saint of England grew out of this. As a supposed officer in the Roman army, later martyred for his faith, St George was an obvious patron for soldiers. All the original Knights had been on the French campaign, and nearly all of them had fought at Crécy. As for the garter, it was perhaps a badge adopted on the spur of the moment by the King's own band of warriors at some episode during the campaign, perhaps at Crécy itself.

The first Knights ranged from some of the most powerful nobles in the kingdom to relatively modest members of Edward III's Household. What they had in common was that they were all loyal, all young and all brave. They were Edward III's personal warrior band, their loyalty reinforced and their valour rewarded by the prestige and glamour which membership of the new Order brought them. Or, to be exact, they were two warrior bands, those of Edward III and his son, the Black Prince, who had had his first experience of fighting in the French campaign. In their chapel at Windsor, the Knights sat facing each other in two rows, with the King on one side and the Black Prince on the other, like opposing teams; it has in fact been suggested that they derived from two teams meeting in friendly rivalry at a tournament, perhaps the great one held at Windsor to celebrate the birth of another son to Edward III in 1348.

Like other fellowships of all types in the Middle Ages, the Garter had a religious and a charitable element. The Poor Knights, military men of good repute but reduced circumstances, were housed and supported at Windsor in return for attending services all the year round, and praying for the souls of the Garter Knights proper. When in church or attending Garter ceremonies, they wore red cloaks, ornamented with the red cross of St George. A College of St George, made up of a Dean, twelve Canons, thirteen Priest-vicars and an establishment of singing-clerks and choirboys, maintained daily services, prayed for the sovereign and the Order and officiated at its ceremonies.

The Order instituted by the brave and dashing King for his equally brave and dashing followers flourished from the start. It was not, as it was often claimed to be, the earliest such Order to be founded; the King of Castile's Order of the Band was about fifty years older. But it soon became so prestigious that in

7 The original west doors of Henry III's chapel at Windsor, now in the east end of St George's Chapel.

8 (right) Looking from the roof of St George's Chapel down to Eton College Chapel.

the fifteen years after 1348 five other Orders were founded in emulation of it all over Europe. Foreign kings and emperors were flattered to be asked to join it; it became a useful way of encouraging or cementing an alliance. The nature of its Knights gradually changed; they became older, on the average grander, and by the sixteenth century were made up of the leading noblemen and statesmen in the kingdom, with a scattering of European royalties.

The buildings, panoply and ceremonies of the Order steadily increased in splendour. All medieval fellowships, from chivalric orders to craftsmen's guilds, needed a place to meet, a place to feast and a place to pray. Edward III built a new Chapter-house, with a Vestry adjoining, and the room that later became known as St George's Hall. He took over and altered the existing castle chapel, a lovely building put up under Henry III, the superb west entrance and doors of which are now incorporated into the east end of St George's Chapel (Pl. 7). Edward IV built this as a new and larger chapel for the Order, perhaps partly as his response to the chapel of Eton College, built by his supplanted predecessor Henry VI down on the plain below the Castle (Pl. 8). It acquired magnificent vestments, plate, tapestries and relics. The Emperor Sigismund celebrated his investiture as a Knight in 1416 by presenting the heart of St George; at various times part of the saint's arm, a bone, a leg (encased in silver armour, with a golden spur) and his head were also acquired. These and other relics, including a fragment of the True Cross, disappeared at the Reformation.

The Knights originally had mantles of blue cloth, and wore a richly embroidered garter, inscribed with the motto of the Order, above their left knee. Blue velvet replaced blue cloth under Henry VI. A chain (known as a "collar") of twenty-four gilt garters joined by gold knots, supporting a jewel-studded representation of St George and the Dragon (the "great George"), was added under Henry VII, along with blue velvet caps decorated with white feathers. All these were for wear at Garter ceremonies. The Garter Star, made up of rays of light emanating from the cross of St George surrounded by a garter, was an innovation of the time of Charles I. It was for every day; up till the end of the eighteenth century, Knights walked the streets or went out hunting with the Garter Star pinned to their breasts.

The mystique and magnificence of the Garter was concentrated into the celebration of its annual feast. It originally took place on and around 23 April,

the feast day of its patron saint, St George. For several centuries it was the most glamorous and prestigious event of the year in England. It involved very large numbers of people, for not only did the entire Court move to Windsor for it, but each Knight usually arrived with an escort of fifty men, and sometimes more.

The Feast, in its original form, went on over three days of services, meetings and banquets. But the most splendid celebration took place on St George's Day, 23 April. The events of the day included three processions, in which monarch, Knights, Poor Knights, Heralds, Officers, Dean, Canons, priests and choir all took part: one down from the King's Presence Chamber to St George's Chapel for the main service, a "grand procession" held in the middle of the service, emerging from the Chapel, doing the circuit of it, and going back in again, and a final procession up to the Royal Lodgings again, for the Feast Day dinner.

Sometimes, "to enlarge the gallantry of the show", the monarch and Knights went on horseback down to the Chapel and back again, but more often they walked, the monarch, preceded by his sword-bearer, under a canopy of cloth of gold carried by twelve Gentlemen of the Privy Chamber (Pl. 9). The Knights brought their own attendants to hold their trains and line the route down to the Chapel. The heart of St George was carried in the "grand procession" under its own cloth of gold canopy. Cloth of gold was everywhere: in canopies, copes and the under-robes of monarch and Knights. Further colour was provided by the blue robes of the Knights, the red cloaks of the Poor Knights and the gay heraldic dress of Garter King of Arms and his associates.

Episodes of the service included the ceremonial kissing by monarch and Knights of St George's heart and arm "decently wrapped up in napkins" and their presentation of gold and silver at the altar. New Knights, if any, were installed. The music and singing, in the church and for the grand procession, were the most splendid that could be devised; and for the final ascent to the Upper Ward for the dinner the royal trumpeters joined the procession, to "sound all the way up ... and as soon as they cease, the Drums and Fifes begin to beat and play".

The monarch retired briefly to the private rooms of his Lodgings, then re-emerged for the dinner in St George's Hall. An engraving in Ashmole's *Order of the Garter* shows, in slightly simplified form, how this was arranged at the time of the book's publication in 1672 (Pl. 10). By then only the monarch and Knights ate at the dinner; in earlier centuries there were further tables for the officers of the Order and any distinguished strangers (or prisoners awaiting ransom in the Castle) who happened to be around. The monarch sat under a canopy at the upper end of the Hall, the Knights along one side of a long table down one side of it. All the royal plate was on show. Sometimes the monarch invited one or more of the more distinguished Knights to sit at the royal table, but Charles II always ate alone. Members of the public, or at least of the Court, were allowed into the main body of the Hall as spectators, although they are not shown by Ashmole; a balustrade was set up at the monarch's end of the Hall, to keep the crowds watching him eat at a distance.

The meal consisted of two courses and a dessert, served to the monarch by twenty or so Gentlemen Pensioners, accompanied by officers of the Household, and to the Knights by the Yeomen of the Guard, while the musicians played from the gallery. The courses were not as we conceive the meaning of the word today: in 1667 each of the King's courses consisted of twenty-nine dishes, ranging from wild-boar pie, haggis puddings and two roasted pigs in the first course to six pheasants with their eggs, pickled oysters and six roasted lobsters in the second. All these fifty-eight dishes were for the King alone; he took what he wanted, and the rest was distributed to members of the Household or the poor, waiting at the Castle gates.

There was an interlude in the meal between the first and second courses. Monarch and Knights rose to their feet; the monarch toasted the Knights and the Knights toasted the monarch. Then Garter King of Arms, followed by his

9 (top right) Charles II in the Grand Procession of the Garter Feast. Detail from the engraving after Wenceslaus Hollar in Ashmole *Order of the Garter* (1672).

10 (bottom right) Ashmole's view of the dinner at the Garter Feast in St George's Hall.

The Prospect of the inside of
S. GEORGES HALL

1 The Soveraign sitting at dinner   2. Knights sitting at dinner   3. Attendants   4. Court Cubberds that serve the Knights Tables   5 Garter principall king of Armes   6 Officers of Armes
7 Treasurer of the Houshold.   8. Controller of the Houshold.   9. Sewer.   10. Pensioners, carrying the second course.   11 Celerer   12. Master of the Houshold.   13. Yeomen of the Guard.

Pag. 503.

heralds and officers at arms, marched into the Hall. He cried out "Largesse", and proclaimed the monarch as "by the Grace of God King of Great Britain, France and Ireland, Defender of the Faith and Sovereign of the Most Noble Order of the Garter" in Latin, French and English. He and all the heralds shouted out "Largesse" again. They were, indeed, asking for a tip. Garter King of Arms held out his hat, and the Treasurer of the Household put the royal gift into it (ten pounds in the time of Charles II). The heralds then retreated backwards out of the Hall, bowing as they went, and went off to their dinner.

Edward III's Hall has been twice re-modelled, and its original appearance is known only from Ashmole's engraving. His Chapter-house was absorbed into the Deanery in the eighteenth or nineteenth century and redecorated as a modern dining-room, so that Victorian deans ate their eggs and bacon where medieval kings used to invest and exhort their Knights (today it is the Dean's drawing-room). But the vaulted Vestry of the Order, next to their Chapter-house, survives, little altered, as the Dean's Chapel (Pl. 11), and Edward III's great sword, six foot four and a quarter inches long, a sword for use, not just ceremony, is on show in the choir of St George's. It was probably hung over his stall when he died.

Edward IV's chapel is the great glory of the medieval fabric of Windsor. Started in about 1475, under the superintendence of Richard Beauchamp, Bishop of Salisbury, and Chancellor of the Order, it was

11 (top left) St George and the Dragon, from a window in the Dean's chapel.

12 (bottom left) The former vestry of the Order of the Garter, now the private chapel in the Deanery.

13 (above) St George's Chapel: the west front.

completed in the reign of Henry VII, over fifty years later. Both kings and Knights contributed to its cost, and their arms or devices figure in the exquisite fan vaulting which is the Chapel's most distinctive feature (Pl. 16). That of Sir Reginald Bray is especially prominent among them. He was a trusted but some thought over-obsequious servant of Henry VII, who was elected to the Garter in 1501. He had derived great wealth from royal favour and passed much of it on to the Chapel before and after his death in 1503. His device was a "hemp-tray" (Pl. 18), an instrument used in the manufacture of hemp; it is nearly as much in evidence on the fabric as the rose, surrounded by rays of light, of Edward IV (Pl. 17). All the Knights contributed to the final section of vaulting, erected over the crossing in 1528, and their arms are carved on it. It was in fact an economy, for the intention had been to erect a tower and lantern over the crossing, but this was given up because of the cost. Monarchs, Knights and Canons were buried in the Chapel in some numbers, and their tombs and chantry chapels form a girdle round it (Pls. 20, 22).

The projects for royal tombs were curiously abortive. Henry VI's has vanished almost without trace. Henry VIII planned to be buried in the old and by then much altered chapel of Henry III, at the east end of St George's. He commandeered the marble sarcophagus from Italy which had been commissioned by Cardinal Wolsey for himself, but his own monument was never completed, and the sarcophagus was later removed to St Paul's Cathedral to contain the body of Admiral Nelson.

14-17 St George's Chapel. (Top) flying buttresses on the south aisle. (Above) looking along the south front. (Top right) fan vaulting in the south choir aisle. The choir was vaulted by the master masons William Vertue and John Hylmer between 1506 and 1508. (Bottom right) Edward IV's device, the rayed rose, carved on a wall of the chapel.

Charles I was buried without ceremony after his execution and plans, under Charles II, to erect a mausoleum for him, to the designs of Christopher Wren, did not come to anything. Even Edward IV never got more than a portion of the tomb for which he left instructions in his will. It was to have consisted of an upper and a lower chapel, with a figure of Death above his grave in the lower chapel and his monument and effigy in the upper chapel. Neither effigy was ever installed; what survive are (in a slightly different position) the miraculously elaborate iron gates which separated off the lower chapel (Pl. 19), and the oriel windows surrounding the upper chapel. In the sixteenth century, this became a royal pew (Pl. 23). There was a separate royal chapel in the Upper Ward, but the pew was used by royal wives as a place from which to watch Garter ceremonies, and one of the stone oriels was replaced, in the reign of Henry VIII, by one of wood, carved with mixed Gothic and Renaissance ornament. A pretty painting by H.E. Dawe shows a wide-eyed Queen Victoria looking down through it as a very young queen (Pl. 24). Wyatville's alterations had destroyed the old Royal Chapel in the Upper Ward, but she complained bitterly about

18 (left) A detail in the south transept. The transept served as the chantry chapel of Sir Reginald Bray, whose device, a hemp-tray, is carved below the angel.

19 (above left) A detail of the iron gates made for the tomb of Edward IV.

20 (above right) The early-sixteenth century tomb of Charles Somerset, 1st Earl of Worcester, KG, and his wife, seen through its surrounding grille.

21 (right) The vault over the crossing. It was put up in 1528 and is decorated with the coats of arms of Henry VII and the Garter Knights, who paid for it.

how cold St George's was, and had a new Private Chapel (Pl. 76) installed as soon as possible.

She was looking down into five hundred years of concentrated chivalry. The choir is the heart of the Order of the Garter (Pl. 28). To left and right of the entrance from the nave are the stalls of monarch and Prince of Wales, followed by the stalls of the Knights. Each stall is surmounted by an elaborate wooden canopy, each canopy is crowned by the helm and sword of the Knight sitting below, and above their helms their multi-coloured banners hang in rows (Pls. 26, 27). Fixed above each seat, glowing with enamel colours and intensely moving in their crowded richness, are the coats of arms of former Knights, dating from the fifteenth century onwards (Pl. 29).

22 (top left) The chantry chapel of John Oxenbridge, Canon of St George's, erected *c*. 1522. The sword of Edward III hangs to the left of the chantry.

23 (bottom left) Looking into the choir of St George's Chapel from Edward IV's chantry chapel, later the Royal Pew.

24 (right) Queen Victoria in the Royal Pew. From an engraving after H.E. Dawe.

25 (below) Looking across the monument to Edward VII and Queen Alexandra, to the Royal Pew.

26 and 27 (top left) Stall canopies, helms and banners of the Knights of the Garter.

28 (bottom left) St George's Chapel: the choir.

29 (above) Coats of arms of past Knights, set into the woodwork above one of the stalls in the choir.

Originally Knights' stalls alternated with Canons' stalls; the latter had lower canopies and the Canons only sat in them at services where the Knights were absent. This odd box-and-cox arrangement largely disappeared when the Canons' stalls were given over to extra Knights and honorary foreign Knights. Two extra stalls were added to either side in the 1780s; they were carved with considerable brio, by Henry Emlyn, an idiosyncratic carpenter-architect living in Windsor, who enriched them with some lively scenes from the life of George III.

George III gave the Chapel a bigger organ and a new choir screen, also designed by Emlyn, to support it. He was one of the post-medieval monarchs who was most committed to Windsor, and to the Garter's presence there. By no means all of them were. Edward VI was suspicious of the Catholic background of the Order, sold most of the Chapel treasures, got rid of St George as its patron saint and re-wrote its statutes. Queen Mary brought St George back, and celebrated the installation of her husband Philip of Spain as a KG with great

30 (above) and 31 (right) Queen Elizabeth, her sword-bearer, and two Knights of the Garter. From a series of engravings after Marcus Gheeraerts, 1578.

splendour at Windsor in 1554, but her reign was too short for her to make much mark on the buildings.

In 1567 Elizabeth did Windsor Castle a serious disservice. Henry VIII had already started moving the Garter Feast from St George's Day if it suited him better. Elizabeth passed an ordinance to the effect that both Feasts and Installations need not be held at Windsor, but could take place wherever it was convenient for the monarch. From then on in her reign most Garter events were held at Whitehall or Greenwich; it is ironic that it was she who commissioned one of the most elaborate visual celebrations of the Order, a series of engravings of herself, the Garter Knights and the Garter officials parading in full robes with the Castle in the background (Pls. 30, 31).

The Stuarts celebrated Garter Feasts at Windsor more often, though never annually. Ashmole praised Charles I as "a great restorer of the ancient Solemnities and Discipline of this Order". Hanging in the Deanery is a painted tree with the arms and titles of the Knight suspended from its branches, all

removable, like pieces in a jigsaw, for replacement when a Knight died (Pl. 32). This was installed in the Chapter-house of the Order under Charles I. The King, with contributions from the Knights, did his best to replace the plate sold by Edward VI — to no avail, for in the Civil War years it was all purloined by a Cromwellian officer. It was replaced in the reign of Charles II, and it is this plate which provides the bulk of that used in the Chapel today.

Charles II's affability, charm and fondness for women did not mean that he was allergic to order or ceremony. He took them with intense seriousness, as a necessary element in the mystique of monarchy. At relevant moments he could assume majesty with grace and conviction, because he believed in it. He loved Windsor because of the pleasant times he could have there, but he was also a favourer and fosterer of its Garter connections. It was in his reign and under his patronage that, in 1672, Elias Ashmole, Windsor Herald at Arms, published his monumental history of the Order. At the time it was published, Garter dinners were still being celebrated in the medieval St George's Hall. In 1678 Charles II re-built the greater part of the Royal Lodgings, decorating the facade which they presented to the outside world with a Garter Star fourteen feet high (Pl. 33). In 1680, he went on to re-model St George's Hall and the adjacent Royal Chapel. John Evelyn had visited Windsor Castle in 1654 and commented on "the rooms, melancholy, and of ancient magnificence". It was taken for granted that the way to uphold the honour of the Garter was to re-model its Hall with modern magnificence, rather than to conserve its ancient appearance.

32 (above) The coat of arms of Charles I, surrounded by replaceable shields and titles of the then Knights of the Garter. One of three panels now in the Deanery Library.

The Hall was re-fashioned, and its walls and ceilings painted with frescoes by Antonio Verrio (Pl. 34). On the ceiling the Muses and other allegorical figures surrounded the Star and collar of the Garter, and in the central oval a cloud-borne Charles II in Garter robes was crowned in glory by angels and cherubs. Along the length of the inner wall Verrio painted Edward III's reception of the Black Prince after Crécy. In the fashion of the time he showed this as a Roman Triumph, with the Prince and his Knights processing in classical armour behind a Corinthian colonnade.

33 (above) The north elevation of the Star Building, erected to the designs of Hugh May in 1675-8 to contain Charles II's new Royal Lodgings.

34 (below) St George's Hall, as re-modelled by Hugh May and frescoed by Antonio Verrio in the 1680s. From the aquatint in Pyne *Royal Residences*.

Later Stuarts remained content with what Charles II had done, and the first Hanoverians took little interest in Windsor, although they came to it occasionally for Garter Installations. George III, however, not only grew to love it but did much for the Garter, although almost all that he did has been replaced or removed. In 1787, he commissioned Benjamin West to paint a series of scenes from the life of Edward III for his Audience Room. (By now, medieval knights could be shown as medieval knights.) Ceiling paintings of St George and the Dragon and episodes from the life of St George, all by Mathew Cotes Wyatt, followed in 1806-9. At the same time M.C. Wyatt's father, James Wyatt, was introducing gothic windows and a gothic staircase into the Royal Lodgings, and father and son were collaborating in turning the never-completed burial chapel of Henry VIII into a new Garter Chapter-house, with a royal burial vault excavated beneath it. Although work on the former continued for a year or two after the King's illness returned in 1811, it was never completed, and the Wyatts' work was later swept away, but the burial vault survives (Pl. 35).

On 23 April 1805, George III had celebrated the Garter Feast at Windsor with a splendour and attention to traditional practices unequalled since the days of Charles II. It was the height of the Napoleonic Wars, and according to a contemporary article nothing could have been "so well calculated to cherish the chivalrous spirit ... which burned in the breast of our ancestors" and to fan "the flame of loyalty and patriotism".

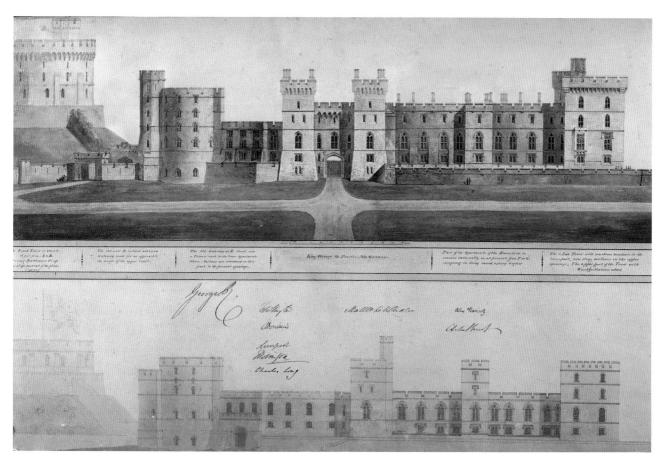

It was in fact the last Garter Feast on the grand scale, and the last Installation until 1948. But celebration had moved from ceremony to architecture. In 1815 Walter Scott, the most popular writer in the British Isles, wrote a poem on the Battle of Waterloo in which he praised England for living up to the standards of its patron "sainted knight":

> Gallant St George, the flower of chivalry
> For thou hast faced, like him, a dragon foe
> And rescued innocence from overthrow

By now the Middle Ages were no longer written off, as they often had been in the eighteenth, and even the seventeenth, centuries, as an age of ignorance and superstition. They had become the Age of Chivalry; its forms and values were worthy of imitation to give inspiration to the present.

So when George IV, not long after his accession to the crown in 1820, asked Parliament for money for Windsor, it was not surprising that he got it, and almost inevitable that the money should be spent on turning it back into a castle. Its restoration was both a celebration of tradition and a symbol of national pride following on victory. Unlike George IV's other building ventures, it was paid for directly by Parliament and supervised jointly by the King and a Parliamentary commission; unlike them the money spent on it provoked

37 (top left) St George's Hall as re-modelled by Wyatville and depicted by Joseph Nash.

38 (far left) The Grand Staircase to St George's Hall and the State Apartments. It was designed by Anthony Salvin to replace Wyatville's staircase.

39 (left) Looking up into the roof of Wyatville's Waterloo Chamber.

40 (above) Louis Philippe being invested in the Garter Throne-room in October 1844. From the watercolour by Louis Haghe.

relatively little criticism (and then only when the original estimate of £155,000 had reached £800,000), and the final result was widely acclaimed.

Four eminent architects were asked to provide designs, and those of Jeffrey Wyatt, James Wyatt's nephew and former assistant, were chosen. He soon changed his name to the more feudal-sounding Wyatville, to go with the re-modelled Castle, and took up residence in the Winchester Tower (Pl. 132), where William of Wykeham had lodged before him when supervising Edward III's building works. Although he had extensive plans for the Lower Ward, his work in the end was almost entirely confined to the Upper Ward and the Round Tower; but this was enough to transform the Castle's image (Pl. 36). All windows were gothicised, crenellations and machicolations replaced plain battlements or flat parapets, bay and oriel windows were protruded, towers were heightened; and overall rose the dominating silhouette of the Round Tower, raised by an extra thirty-three feet. It is possible to be less enthusiastic than his contemporaries were about Wyatville's often tame or over-scaled detail; but the silhouette is a triumph.

Although there was less Gothic inside than Wyatville wanted, even in the decoration of the rooms which were not gothicised the Garter was much in evidence; and one sequence of state was provided that was lavishly neo-medieval. A vaulted Gothic entrance hall, a Gothic staircase (later re-modelled by Salvin; Pl. 38) and guard-room hung with medieval armour, led to a St

39

I have fought the good fight. I have finished my course. II · TIM · IV · 7.

George's Hall doubled in size, gothicised and decorated with the shields of all past and present members of the Garter (Pl. 37). Next to the Hall, the new Waterloo Chamber (Pl. 39) was hung with Lawrence's portraits of those who had contributed to the downfall of Napoleon. Modern victory, ancient chivalry and royal magnificence were deliberately combined.

George IV died before these rooms were completed. Under William IV and Queen Victoria state banquets and Garter events returned to Windsor (Pl. 40), and beneath tiers of gold plate the Queen presided over huge dinners in St George's Hall. But Windsor during her reign acquired a more personal tribute to chivalry. She saw her husband as a modern knight. She had him depicted in armour both during his lifetime and after his death. Before his body was removed to the mausoleum at Frogmore, it rested for nearly a year in George III's uncompleted Garter Chapter-house. In celebration of this, and to provide a building which, unlike the mausoleum, was open to the public the Chapter-house was converted into an Albert Memorial Chapel. Gilbert Scott devised sumptuous decoration and Baron de Triqueti carved a monument in white marble ("as pure and as free from blemish as his own blameless life", the newspapers said), in which he was shown in full medieval armour, wearing his Garter insignia and with his greyhound Eos at his feet (Pl. 41).

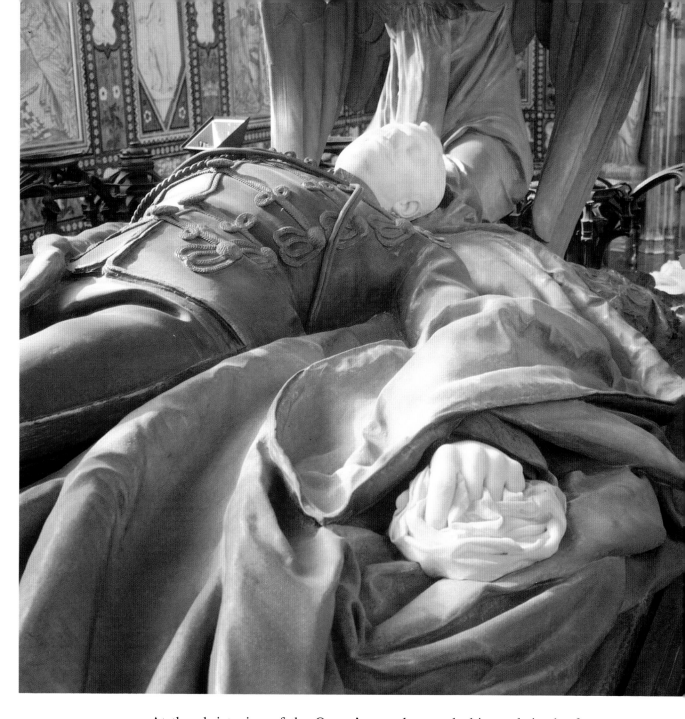

At the christening of the Queen's grandson and ultimate heir, the future Duke of Clarence, in 1864, the Queen's present to him consisted of another effigy of the Prince Consort as a knight. Suitable inscriptions encouraged the infant prince to model himself on his grandfather. He had shown no signs of doing so when he died unexpectedly of pneumonia in 1891; but in a memorial by Alfred Gilbert put up to him in the Albert Memorial Chapel he is depicted, movingly if a little inappropriately, as a modern young knight who lies dead, sword in hand, on the battlefield (Pl. 42).

42 A detail from Alfred Gilbert's monument to the Duke of Clarence, also in the Albert Memorial Chapel.

The annual Garter celebration at Windsor, defunct since the sixteenth century, was renewed in modified form in 1948. It involves a procession to the Chapel (Pl. 43), a ceremony at which new Knights are installed, and a luncheon, held in the Waterloo Chamber. It seems sad that this does not take place in St George's Hall; the reason may be that Wyatville's ambitious enlargement has made it too big for the scale of the modern luncheon. Perhaps changes following on the 1992 fire will make it possible to bring it back again.

43 (above) The Garter Procession today.

44 (right) The children of George III, with Queen's Lodge and Windsor Castle in the background. Detail from a portrait by Benjamin West. The princes are wearing the Windsor uniform, designed by George III for his family and senior Household, and still worn at Windsor today.

3 Lodging the Monarch

(Pictura ista inferius locata, uti et symbola
cum in hâc paginâ, tum in adversâ exacte
ab exemplaria in imtio libri origni limantur.
Vide aliam picturam fol. 71. b. postea.)

Secratis: Edere oportet ut vivas non vivere ut edas

Rex erit invictus fuerit cui copia victus

Almoniam super omnia populi plus requirunt. Sineca

45 King Edward IV at table. From a seventeenth-century copy of *Domus Regie Magnificencie*, regulations for the royal Household, written in about 1470.

How does, or should, a king live? Not surprisingly, royal needs and attitudes have changed over the centuries, and Windsor has changed with them. Royal lifestyles can be disinterred from it, layer by layer. Even though the nineteenth-century layer is the dominating one, it has been affected by what happened before and has happened since. Under all the alterations, much of the structure of the Upper Ward goes back to the thirteenth and fourteenth centuries, and in what are now called the State Apartments one can still get the feel of Charles II's Royal Lodgings and savour how differently his life was organised from that of George IV or, even more, of Queen Victoria.

Charles II's way of living came at the end of a development which had started well back into the Middle Ages. It had nothing to do with domesticity,

44

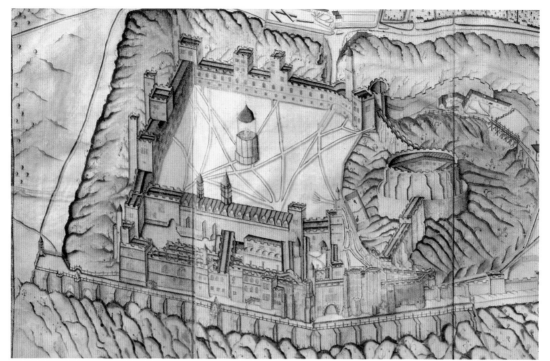

or with the family except as a political tool. The king married his queen for political or dynastic reasons, not for love. Each had matching but quite separate suites of rooms, and separate servants to go with them. They shared no rooms in common. They seldom ate or slept together. Their children were brought up separately, and only met their parents at long intervals. The Prince of Wales, in particular, as heir to the throne, had his own establishment not all that much smaller than those of his parents, and was treated as a little adult; Charles II was initiated as a Knight of the Garter, in miniature mantle, cap and robes, at the age of seven.

Royal lifestyle was tied up with royal power. Power had to be maintained, against threats from foreign monarchs or powerful nobles at home. At a working level, since there was no distinction from the Middle Ages up to the seventeenth century between the place where someone lived and the place where he worked, the royal lodgings were also, in modern terms, the royal office, the place where the king maintained his power by receiving messengers and ambassadors, taking counsel and giving orders; and it was taken for granted that this activity should happen in virtually all the rooms occupied by the king, including his bedroom.

But power could be bolstered by the right image. Lavishness, ceremony and mystery all contributed. Lavishness suggested the wealth of a king, who could feed large numbers of people, or be served with far more food than he needed, or set himself off with costly fabrics, rich architecture and displays of gold plate. Ceremony underlined the fact that he was different from, and superior to, other men (Pl. 45); it could involve every action of the day, from his getting up and dressing to his going to bed. Mystery, by keeping him secret and hard of access, made his public appearances more dramatic, and gave a sense of privilege to those who were allowed to penetrate into the secret places. But it

45

could be overdone; kings who were never seen always got into trouble.

All these different aspects got mixed up together. In very early days royal lodgings consisted of a Hall, where the king's servants ate and lived, and he himself ate when he gave great feasts, and a Chamber, for his everyday sleeping, eating and conducting of business. But the Chamber gradually hived off a sequence of more and more rooms, partly because habits became more sophisticated and luxurious, partly because the pressure of people wanting access to the king made each successive room less private and encouraged the king to retreat to a new one. Something not far removed from the basic hall-and-chamber system may have existed in the first days of Windsor Castle. When Henry III finally settled the king's quarters

47 (above) The Henry VII wing, added to the Royal Lodgings in about 1497-9.

48 (top right) Queen Elizabeth's Gallery, as converted into the Royal Library.

49 (right) The chimneypiece installed in the Gallery in 1583.

in the Upper Ward and re-modelled the existing Royal Lodgings there, he provided something a good deal more elaborate. King's and Queen's Lodgings of several rooms adjoined a hall and chapel, all built around the two courtyards that later became known as the Brick and Horn Courts (Pl. 46). The hall and chapel filled the space occupied today by St George's Hall as it was to be enlarged by Wyatville, but the exact plan and arrangements of the remainder can only be surmised.

In 1485 Henry VII founded the Yeomen of the Guard, partly for extra security, partly for prestige. In the King's Lodgings they took over the first room after the hall, the Great Chamber, where up till then the king had eaten when in public, and it was re-named the Watching-chamber or Guard-chamber accordingly. This infiltration of a new function had a knock-on effect in the sequence, and meant that it had to be extended at the far end. The result at

46

Windsor was that a short new wing appeared at the north-west corner, probably containing a bedchamber, inner chamber and closet on the main floor (Pl. 47). The wing was in the latest fashion, and its most conspicuous features were two elaborate bay windows, like fancy lanterns or expanding concertinas of glass and stone, that are also to be found in Henry VII's chapel at Westminster Abbey. It was altered by Wyatville, but is still recognisable.

The next addition was the result of another new fashion, brought over from France, for galleries in which to take exercise and hang portraits. Edward VI had complained that at Windsor "methinks I am in prison ... here be no galleries, nor no gardens to walk in". Elizabeth remedied the defect in 1582-4 by adding a wing containing a gallery to Henry VII's building; it is now, much re-decorated,

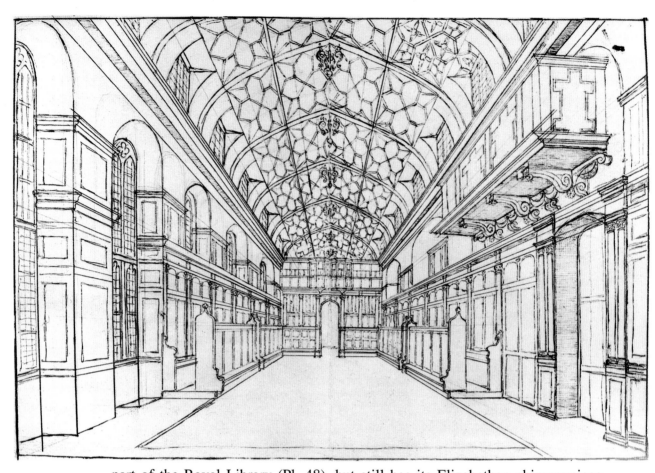

50 (above) The Royal Chapel, as re-modelled by Queen Elizabeth in 1570-71. From a drawing by Wenceslaus Hollar.

51 (right) The Henry III Tower. It retains the only surviving example of the distinctive windows inserted throughout the Upper Ward to the designs of Hugh May under Charles II.

part of the Royal Library (Pl. 48), but still has its Elizabethan chimneypiece (Pl. 49). For out-of-doors walking she built a long terrace along the north front of the Royal Lodgings, rising sheer out of the hillside in a way that evoked the marvel of contemporaries. It replaced a much less substantial timber walk which Henry VIII had had built, and where he used to practise shooting with a crossbow. Elizabeth took regular exercise on her terrace when she was at Windsor, rain or fine, but not when it was windy; her hair arrangements were probably too vulnerable.

The Queen also re-modelled the Royal Chapel, in 1570-71 (Pl. 50), and even if she did not keep Garter Feasts at Windsor she spent a good deal of time there; but she did not love it as Charles II came to. He used it as a place for summer holidays, and spent happy months there. The poet Thomas Otway wrote of it as:

> ... that Majestic Pile, where oft his Care
> A while forgot he might for Ease repair
> A seat for sweet Retirement, Health, and Love

The King seems to have fallen for its attractions when the Court spent two months of the summer of 1670 there, and, according to the *London Gazette*, were "extremely satisfied with the pleasantness of that princely seat". After that he came most summers. He loved outdoor life, walked, rode, and hunted in the parks, fished in the Thames and organised horse-races in the water meadows at Datchet. All this looked after Health; and Love was not forgotten either.

One result of these summer stays was that the Royal Lodgings were re-modelled and partially re-built, between 1675 and 1684. The architect was Christopher Wren's deputy Hugh May, who was Comptroller of the Works at Windsor. In the 1670s Gothic was out of fashion; but May or the King, or both, must have thought that the new work should respect its context, and it was given a fortress air, with occasional battlements and windows curiously set back inside deep, round-headed recesses. A fragment of this treatment survives, on the King Henry III Tower (Pl. 51), to the south-west of the Round Tower.

Inside, fortress severity gave way to up-to-date luxury: tapestries, hangings and furniture of great richness were set off by ceilings frescoed by Antonio Verrio, and luscious carvings

of fruit and flowers by Grinling Gibbons (Pls. 34, 52-3, 55-6). In plan, however, the slightly re-modelled Lodgings were a more elaborate version of the traditional formula. On the King's side the sequence ran as follows: Guard-room, Presence Chamber, Privy Chamber, Withdrawing-room, Great Bedchamber, Little Bedchamber, Closet, with an Eating-room to one side of the main axis. Only Withdrawing-room, Little Bedchamber and Eating-room were new arrivals since the sixteenth century. The Queen had a similar, but slightly different sequence.

There were similar sets of rooms at all late Stuart palaces. From contemporary references and directives issued by the king, one can get a good idea of how they were used. The sequence worked as a linear filter, by which access could be controlled (Pl. 54). The first two rooms were easy to get into. The Yeomen of the Guard standing in picturesque attitudes in their colourful dress only had to keep out the lower classes, for anyone who looked like a gentleman or lady was allowed to go through the Wardroom into the Presence Chamber: Charles II specified "all persons or gentlemen of quality and good fortune" and "all wives and daughters of the nobility, and their women that attend them ...

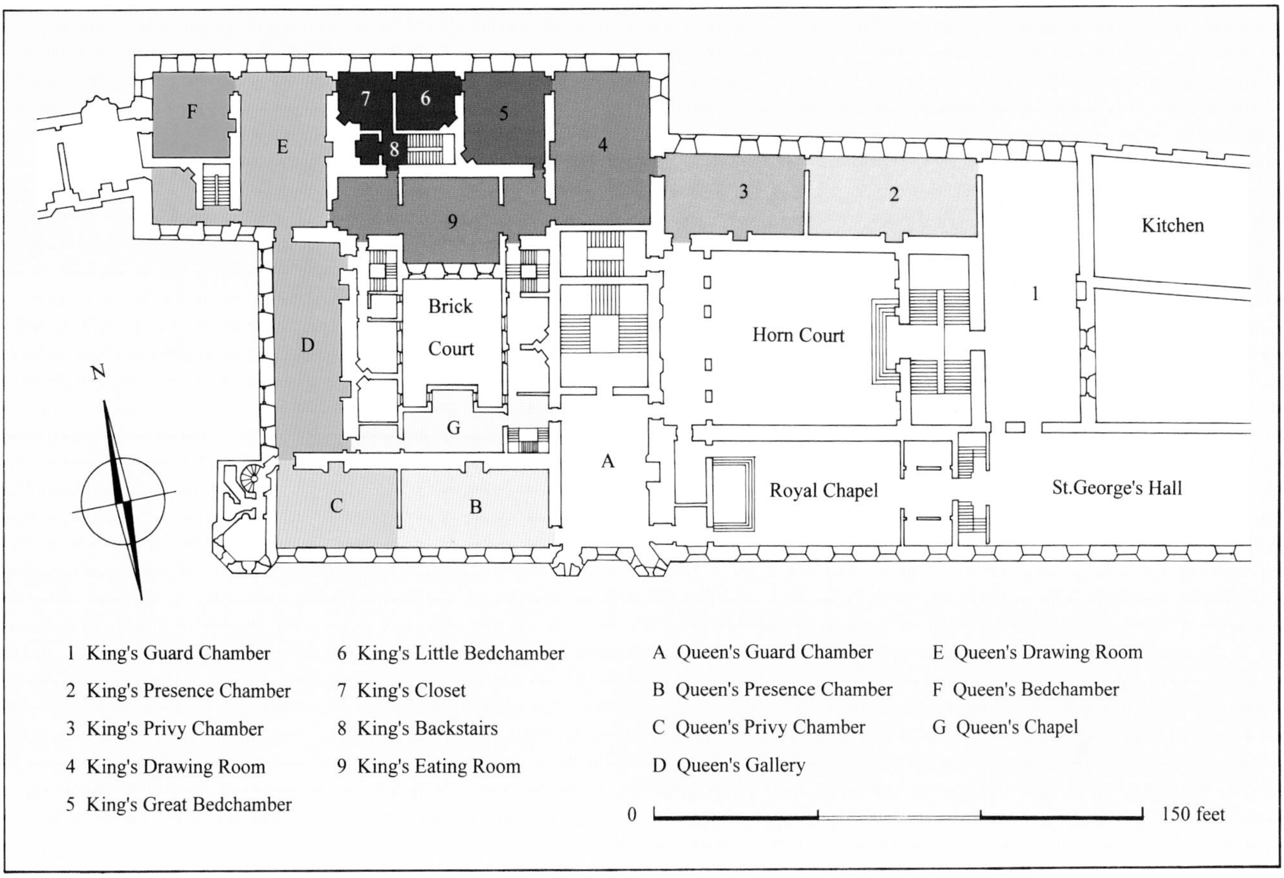
F
E
7
6
5
4
8
3
2
Kitchen
9
1
Brick
Court
Horn Court
N
D
G
A
Royal Chapel
St.George's Hall
C
B
1 King's Guard Chamber
2 King's Presence Chamber
3 King's Privy Chamber
4 King's Drawing Room
5 King's Great Bedchamber
6 King's Little Bedchamber
7 King's Closet
8 King's Backstairs
9 King's Eating Room
A Queen's Guard Chamber
B Queen's Presence Chamber
C Queen's Privy Chamber
D Queen's Gallery
E Queen's Drawing Room
F Queen's Bedchamber
G Queen's Chapel
0
150 feet

52 (top left) The Royal Chapel as re-modelled under Charles II. In the early nineteenth century it was demolished to make way for an enlarged St George's Hall.

53 (bottom left) Grinling Gibbons carving in the King's Eating or Dining Chamber.

54 (above) The Royal Lodgings in the time of Charles II. King's Lodgings are shown blue, Queen's Lodgings red, and the colour coding darkens as the rooms grow harder of access.

and all other ladies of good rank and quality, but not their servants". The Presence Chamber was well supplied with Gentlemen Ushers and Gentlemen Waiters, who were directed to expel "any persons not meet or worthy to be therein".

Visiting ladies and gentlemen, besides being allowed in just to have a look, could also come in to watch the king receiving a deputation in the Presence Chamber, or eating a public dinner there. Eating on occasion in state but also in public (even if a limited public) was considered an important role of the monarch. He carried out both functions seated under the canopy or "state" which dominated one end of the room.

One can watch the filter system at work when the ambassador of the King of Bantam, in the East Indies, came to present letters of credence to the king on 16 May, 1682. He arrived with a troop of lancers and two ceremonial umbrellas, one for himself and one for his letter. He was received in the Presence

Chamber; the attendants carrying the two umbrellas were allowed to "come and stand within the Presence door", but the "ordinary servants with their lances" had to stay in the Guard-room.

The door between the Presence and Privy Chambers technically marked the beginning of the Privy Lodgings, and the realm of a different body of Household officers, run by the Groom of the Stole. By the reign of Charles II the Privy Chamber itself, by the process of infiltration, had become a kind of intermediate zone between Presence Chamber and Privy Lodgings. There was a canopy set up in it as well, and it was used for audiences rather more privileged than that offered to the ambassador of Bantam. The king no longer ate there in private, but used the Eating-room instead. His Household officers sometimes played cards there.

The main Privy Apartments consisted of four rooms, the Withdrawing-room, the Bedchamber, the Small Bedchamber and Closet. The first two were not private at all, in our sense of the word. Access to the Withdrawing-room (soon to drop the "with") was much less limited by the time the Windsor drawing-rooms were fitted up than it had been at the beginning of Charles II's reign, though it was still more select than the Presence Chamber. It had become a room of general resort for those with positions at Court, or for "people of quality" who wished to pay their respects and assembled every morning to meet the king or queen; this social occasion was later to be formalised and described as the holding of a Drawing-room. Right of access to the adjacent Bedchamber was much more limited, but included "the Lord Steward, Lord Chamberlain, the Secretaries of State, the rest of the Lords and other of our Privy Council".

Besides talking or conferring with these great people, Charles II listened to sermons in his Bedchamber, and occasionally ate there; and in 1675 it was there that he knighted Sir Samuel Morland, to celebrate Morland's achievement in bringing a pumped water supply to the Castle. At night the Grooms in waiting slept in the Withdrawing-chamber, the Gentleman in waiting in the Bedchamber. It was the job of the latter, and the Groom of the Stole, both of whom were peers of the realm, to dress the king in the morning.

But did the king sleep in the Bedchamber, or in the Small Bedchamber

adjoining (which certainly by 1696, in the time of William III, was being called the "king's customary bedchamber")? The usual process of rooms becoming more public was clearly causing a second Bedchamber to hive off from the original one, and by the eighteenth century the only use of the bed in the king's first or State Bedchamber was probably to look good, and to lay him out on after his death; but it is not clear whether matters had gone this far under Charles II.

Whether used all or only some of the time, the second Bedchamber was in the same world as the adjacent Closet, differing in terms of size, furnishing, access and atmosphere from the adjacent rooms (Pl. 58). Even though they have been substantially re-decorated since Charles II's day, these rooms still have an air of greater intimacy, due partly to their smaller size and proportions, partly to the smaller size of the pictures with which they are hung. The Closet was the last and most intimate of the royal sequence, the only one to which even Princes of the Blood had no right of access, a room for private meetings of all kinds, political or personal, where the king kept his most exquisite and precious possessions. It, and probably the second Bedchamber also, were rooms in which ceremony was reduced to a minimum; there is a description of King Charles and the Duke of York chatting with their courtiers in the Queen's Closet in 1669, "seeking relief from more weighty cares, and divesting themselves awhile of the restraint of royalty".

Both rooms were in the domain of the Backstairs. This little private

staircase came up behind them, and gave access on the floor below (at least by 1688, as we know from an inventory of that year) to the king's Bedchamber and Eating-room "below stairs".

In all palaces of that period the nest of little rooms around the Backstairs was useful for secret politics, but also for an aspect of the monarchy which was always recognised, the king's need to "divest himself of the restraint of royalty". That, in Charles II's case, this involved a voracious sex life is probably the one fact that most people know about him. This side of him was remarkable only for its excess. It was taken for granted that any king, having married for reasons of state, might want to take a mistress or mistresses; the resulting relationship was semi-official and no attempt was made to keep it secret. Not infrequently, one or more of the mistresses would be appointed one of the Queen's Ladies of the Bedchamber, a situation which caused Charles II's Queen, Catherine of Braganza, great unhappiness when it first occurred but which she later became reconciled to, and which George II's Queen Caroline was to accept with equanimity. According to Pepys, Catherine of Braganza used to make herself heard before going into her own dressing-room, for fear that she would surprise the King carrying on with one of her ladies.

At Windsor, Charles II's favourite mistress the Duchess of Portsmouth had an apartment immediately under his own, with access to it by the Backstairs. Nell Gwynn lived with her royal bastards in Burford House, at the bottom of the hill immediately below the Castle, and it was easy for the King to walk out of the private gate of the Upper Ward and down the hill to her, if he felt like it (Pl. 59).

The little suite of king's Bedchamber and Eating-room "below stairs", listed in 1688, marked the first stage in the making of a distinction between where the monarch lived and where he or she ceremonially worked or politically performed, between their public and private life. It was carried a stage further at Windsor by Queen Anne.

While she was still Princess she had bought a small early-seventeenth century house just below the "rubbish-gate" on the south side of the Castle, so-called because it was effectively the back-door to the Upper Ward. She

enlarged it as a comfortable residence for herself and her husband, and even when she became queen seems to have preferred it to the Royal Lodgings in the Castle. It became known as the Garden House. As Pote, the historian of Windsor, put it in 1755, "after her accession to the throne, when her majesty constantly resided at Windsor every summer, [she] would daily withdraw from the Royal Lodgings, and the state and splendour of a great and victorious Court, to enjoy a happy retirement in this Home and Garden".

George I and II seldom visited Windsor, perhaps only for Garter ceremonies. When they did come, they seem to have slept in the Garden House; but it is recorded that George II continued the tradition of dining in public in the Castle, although he used Charles II's Eating-room, rather than the Presence Chamber.

With George III, a new era started for the Castle. It took some time to get under way. In 1766 a visitor commented: "It hurts one to see almost the only place in England worthy to be styled our King's Palace so totally neglected." In 1776 George III took over the Garden House; as he put it in a letter, "the Queen expressed a strong wish that, as Queen Anne had lived there, I would give it to her; this will give us the means of some pleasant jaunts to that beautiful park".

Unlike many kings, George III loved his wife, and was faithful to her; he called her the "Queen of my heart". In London he had acquired Buckingham House, at the end of the Mall, and given it to her as her own home. The seat of

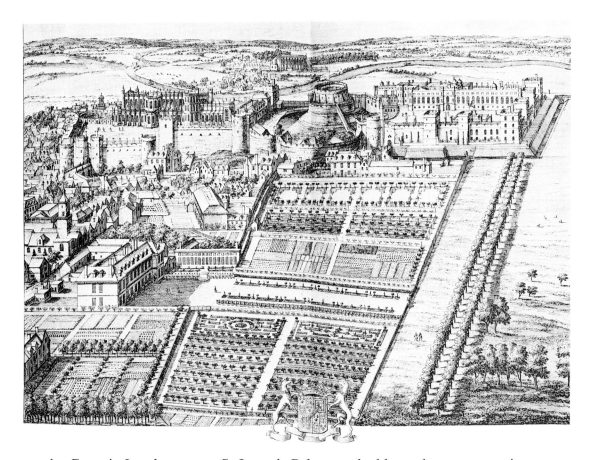

the Court in London was at St James's Palace, as had been the case ever since Whitehall Palace was destroyed by fire in 1698. But George III preferred to sleep in Buckingham House (or the Queen's House, as it became known), and go over to St James's Palace for his ceremonial and official life. His Levée took place in the afternoon and had lost all connection with his getting up in the morning.

At Windsor, the original intention had been to use the Garden House for one-night stays, when the King came over with the Queen for a day's hunting and it was awkward to go back to London or Kew that evening. But they grew increasingly fond of Windsor, stayed there for longer periods and ended up by re-building the Garden House on a larger scale; it then became known as the Queen's Lodge. They used it in the same way they used Buckingham House in London, and the Royal Apartments in the Castle in the same way as those at St James's Palace — but more rarely, for the ceremonial and official life at Windsor was much more limited. Effectively, they built a house to live in, from which to look at Windsor Castle, thirty yards or so away. George III is said to have been his own architect; certainly the almost featureless Queen's Lodge, dumped like a couple of abandoned railway carriages along one side of the Castle, would have reflected no credit on an architect (Pls. 44, 60).

The next stage was to amalgamate this new pattern of public and private life into one building, by moving the private apartments of the Queen's Lodge into the Castle. There were abortive plans to do this as early as 1789, but it

59 (above)
Windsor Castle
from the south,
from the engrav-
ing in Kip
*Britannia
Illustrata.*

56

was not until 1800 that George III finally gave instructions to James Wyatt, his architect, to fit up private apartments for himself and his family in the Castle. Rooms for the Queen and her daughters were created in the east wing of the Upper Ward, and a separate set for the King under the old Royal Lodgings. In effect it was an expanded version of the 1688 "below stairs" apartment, but filled the whole of the ground floor of the Star Building. The work went on at the same time as Wyatt's partial gothicisation of the Upper Ward and Royal Apartments, and the King and Queen moved in in November 1804. The Queen wrote to Lady Harcourt: "Not to shock you or Lord Harcourt with my opinion on this subject I will briefly tell you that I have changed from a very comfortable and warm habitation to the coldest house, room and passages that ever existed."

George III combined belief in the dignity and importance of his office with personal directness and lack of pretension. He had a feeling for the privacy of his home, but very little for that of his surroundings. Almost everything out of doors was freely open to the public, and the King was accessible to anybody there. He and his wife wandered round Windsor looking into the shops; Charles Knight, the owner of a bookshop in the town, came into it one day and found the King, browsing through a copy of Paine's *Rights of Man* which had just come in.

Knight's son, also Charles, describes how he played in the Home Park, the Upper Ward and on the terrace as a boy, and how "the park was a glory for cricket and kite flying. The King would stand alone to see the boys at cricket; and many a time had he bidden us good morning, when we were looking for mushrooms in the early dew and he was returning from his dairy to his eight o'clock breakfast. Everyone knew that most respectable and amiable of country squires, and His Majesty knew everyone ... The King and his family were forever in the public eye. There was a lawn behind the Lodge, but there was no other place in which strangers or neighbours might not gaze upon them or jostle them."

The social event at which the royal family were most in evidence was the daily promenade on the terraces. Promenading in a particular place at a particular time "to see and be seen" was a social habit which had been common all over Europe since at least the seventeenth century, and royalty took part without arousing comment. In London Charles II had started the custom of walking up and down on the Mall, and the Hanoverians continued it. At Windsor a band played on the East Terrace every day except Tuesday and Saturday. Anyone could join the promenade, and the King and Queen took part in it whenever they were in residence (Pl. 61). On most days it was only the townspeople and Castle residents who were involved; but Sundays developed into special occasions when grand people drove in from all over the neighbouring countryside, or down from London, and the waiting queue of their horses and carriages stretched far down into the town.

In 1811 George III's madness (if madness it was) finally overpowered him; he retired into his apartment in the north range, and stayed there for the rest of his life, to most people no more than a lost face occasionally seen in the window. His son took over as Regent, and in 1820 as King. In terms of the image of the Castle, his reign was to be the most important since that of Edward III.

His style differed completely from that of his father (Pl. 60). He was vain, extravagant, grotesque, spoilt and ridiculous, but could charm anyone and everyone when he set his mind to it. He often infuriated his servants and ministers, yet they grew genuinely fond of him, perhaps because he wanted to be loved and was so obviously vulnerable. His infidelities, extravagance and resistance to change brought him great unpopularity during much of his reign; but he loved beautiful things, had a passion for building and collecting, and was a more effective patron than any post-medieval king except Charles I.

60 (above) George IV standing in a costume of his own design before his remodelled castle. From a contemporary engraving.

61 (above right) George III promenading in public on the south terrace at Windsor. The Queen's Lodge, where up to 1800 George III lived in preference to the Castle, can be seen on the left.

On his father's death in 1820, he had to decide what to do about the Castle. After some years of indecision, in 1823 he moved into it for a short trial period, not into his father's apartments in the north range, however, but into those formerly occupied by his mother and sisters. He demolished the Queen's Lodge, which blocked the view from his windows, and closed the terraces except on Sundays, for the sake of privacy. The Dean and Canons were furious about the closure; the townspeople were not happy, but consoled themselves with the thought of the trade and importance that a resident king as extravagant and ebullient as George IV would bring to the town.

The King quickly decided, with some reason, that the Castle as it stood was altogether inadequate as the main royal residence out of London; as related in the previous chapter, in 1824 he went to Parliament for money and got it, along with a "committee of taste" to supervise the way in which it was spent.

The Chancellor of the Exchequer, in pressing the need for the "embellishment and improvement" of the State Apartments, claimed that "nobody would deny that they ought to be maintained with a degree of splendour that was becoming the sovereign who ruled over the country, and also the country over

which he ruled." As Princess Lieven, the sharp-tongued wife of the Russian ambassador, remarked, the King was delighted, and the country could afford to pay: "English finances are magnificent. There has not been such internal prosperity for thirty years." Under the dual banner of splendour and convenience, and with full Parliamentary backing as an expression of national power and wealth, the great project of reconstruction moved ahead (Pls. 62-4). Wyatville was chosen as architect, partly because his plan was so obviously convenient, partly because, as he himself put it, his designs were made "under a most ardent impression to add to the magnificence of the Castle".

The basic concept had in fact been set up under George III. Distinct State and Private Apartments were to be provided in the same building. The challenge was, to make the State Apartments more magnificent, and the Private Apartments more spacious and luxurious, to join the two conveniently together and dispose both so that they were suited to royal needs in the early nineteenth century.

These had changed. In addition to the traditional audiences and banquets, there was a new need for big balls and receptions, such as had been developing in grand houses of all kinds during the late eighteenth and early nineteenth centuries. The monarch had to be able to put these on with at least as much magnificence as his richest subjects, and preferably with more. He could not be outdone by Chatsworth. Such entertainments called for at least three large rooms, conveniently linked together and appropriately decorated: a room for dancing, a room for eating and a room for cards and conversation. The old Royal Apartments were neither big enough nor conveniently enough arranged for this kind of entertainment, with the exception of the King's Guard-room and St George's Hall, and these were too much out on a limb from the rest; although George III had used the Guard-room on occasions as a ballroom, it was inappropriately decorated for this purpose.

The Private Apartments, too, had a relatively new function, which also related to what had been developing in private houses. They had to cater for house-parties. The idea of inviting a selected group of family and friends to a house in the country for a recreational stay of several days duration had only existed in embryo in England (or anywhere else, for that matter) before the mid-eighteenth century, but since then it had been developed to heights of convenience and luxury which made it the admiration of Europe. A formal drawing-room to assemble in before and after dinner, a big dining-room, a library for informal sitting around in, sitting-rooms for the host and hostess to retreat to, and plenty of well-appointed guest bedrooms were the basic accommodation without which no good house-party could take place.

As Prince of Wales, and later Prince Regent, George IV had his own house-parties in the Pavilion at Brighton and the Royal Lodge in Windsor Great Park, in houses in which the traditional royal apparatus of Guard-room, Presence and Privy or Audience Chambers were absent; and he was often the guest of honour at house-parties at Belvoir, Chatsworth and elsewhere. Here too he had to be able to compete with what these grand houses had to offer.

Wyatville dealt with and answered all these questions. He cannot claim all the credit, however. George IV relied heavily for advice in matters artistic and architectural on Sir Charles Long, later created Lord Farnborough, a minor politician so self-effacing that his name has been almost entirely forgotten, but a man of taste and discrimination. It was Long who had master-minded the King's sumptuous coronation in 1821. In 1824 he wrote a memorandum about Windsor Castle which suggested almost everything that was finally done. Wyatville's achievement was to work out his suggestions with professional competence rather than inspiration.

Up till now the only approach of any dignity to the Royal Apartments of Windsor was through the town, into the Lower Ward, up past the Round Tower and through the so-called Norman Gate (in fact fourteenth-century) into the Upper Ward. Wyatville, on Long's suggestion, continued the Long Walk straight up to the south front and made a new gatehouse and gateway there, exactly op-posite the entrance to the Royal Apartments, so that a single magnificent axis now connected this entrance to the end of the Broad Walk, three miles away, where a statue of George III on horseback was erected to close the vista.

A tower was built over the entrance to form one of the newly fashionable portes-cochères, where carriages could disgorge their occupants under cover. A vaulted hall led to a new Grand Staircase, formed by filling in the Brick Court. At the top of this two alternatives were available. To the north the Eating-room became a "Grand Ante-Room" giving access at either end to the King's and Queen's Drawing-rooms, re-decorated for a levée or a "Drawing-room"; the bed-rooms had been got rid of, but a King's and Queen's Closet had been retained, for private audiences before or after a Drawing-room. To the east there was access into a Grand Vestibule where the staircase had been, and then either directly into the Waterloo Chamber, or by way of an enlarged Queen's Guard-room into St George's Hall (Pl. 65), now doubled in size by getting rid of the Royal Chapel. The Waterloo Chamber was a top-lit room formed by filling in the Horn Court, and Lawrence's Waterloo portraits hung there (Pl. 66); the King's Guard-room had been completely re-decorated as what soon became known as the Grand Reception Room. The resulting three very large rooms, all communicating with each other, could deal with almost any grand eventuality. Off the Grand Reception Room Wyatville amalgamated the King's Presence Chamber and Privy Chamber to form a Throne-room, later to be known as the Garter Throne-room, because it was used for Garter investitures and meetings.

In front of the east range a new garden was formed, with a raised terrace all the way round it (Pl. 67). There was an orangery under part of this; the or-ange trees were given by Louis XVIII, and brought up the Thames to Windsor. Inside the east range was filled with a new range of much bigger Private Apartments: a dining-room, drawing-room, library, smaller drawing-room and personal suites for king and potential queen. The sequence continued round the corner into the south range, with more rooms for family or guests. The former apartments in these ranges had been connected by narrow passages, if at all, and had only a tortuous link with the north range. One of the major features of Wyatville's work (again based on a suggestion by Long) was a spacious corridor, fifteen feet wide, built out into the Upper Ward, and running all the way along east and south ranges.

The Corridor may have been inspired by the gallery at the Brighton Pavilion, which was used as a kind of general sitting-room by guests; but it was a great deal longer, and lined all the way with pictures, fine furniture and beautiful objects. It was, and remains, perhaps the most attractive feature of the Private Apartments ("What a place for walky-walky", commented the civil ser-vant and man-about-town Thomas Creevey). At the angle of the two ranges it took a diagonal cut, in order to allow for the sovereign's private entrance hall and private staircase. At the north end of the east range it linked onto St George's Hall; and a new gallery from the Dining-room to the Grand Reception Room provided another link with the State Apartments.

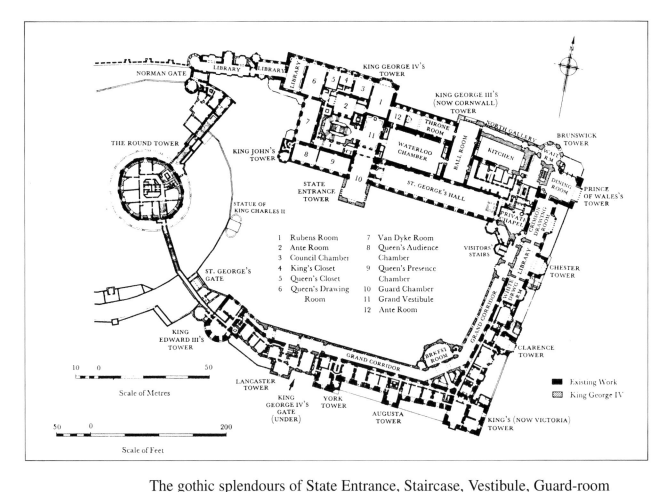

The gothic splendours of State Entrance, Staircase, Vestibule, Guard-room and St George's Hall were in keeping with Wyatt's neo-feudal exterior. But although George IV was by no means averse to Gothic, his particular tastes were to be found more in the Grand Reception Room and Private Apartments, other than the Dining-room. He liked marble and bronze, sumptuousness and glitter, rich fabrics and plenty of gilding, elaborate curtains, huge chandeliers, superlative craftsmanship and superbly patterned carpets, and set in and set off by all this the richest French furniture, or furniture in the French style, and pictures of the best quality glowing in richly gilt frames. All this was to be found in the suite of three rooms on the east front, each given a distinctive colour by the dominant colour of their fabrics: the Crimson Drawing-room, the Green Library (which was later also made a drawing-room), and the White Drawing-room. But the liveliest of his new rooms at Windsor was undoubtedly the Grand Reception Room. In contrast to the static splendour of the Drawing-rooms, it was a room alight with excitement and movement, a brilliant re-creation of the Louis Quinze style, incorporating panelling of that period, set off with swirling plasterwork and lit up at night with a double enfilade of chandeliers (Pl. 70).

These rooms had little if anything to do with Wyatville. "Old French boiserie", he wrote, "would never have appeared in the Castle had the architect been guided solely by his own judgement." It is something of a mystery who was responsible for the Grand Reception Room; but the Private Apartments

62 (above) Plan of the State and Private Apartments as re-modelled by Wyatville.

63 and 64 The Upper Ward and Round Tower, before (top right) and after (bottom right) Wyatville's alterations, 1823-40. From illustrations in Pyne *Royal Residences* (1819) and Nash *Windsor Castle* (1848).

62

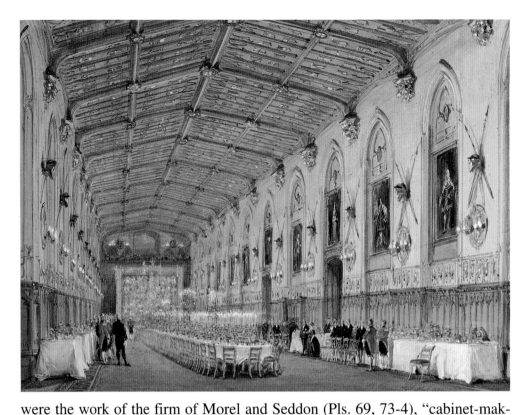

were the work of the firm of Morel and Seddon (Pls. 69, 73-4), "cabinet-makers and upholsterers" by profession, but in effect what today would be called decorators. In 1827 the firm brought in A.C. Pugin and his fifteen-year-old son Augustus Welby Pugin, as Gothic experts to help with the Dining-room (Pl. 68), which unlike the Drawing-rooms was gothic; in later life Welby Pugin dismissed his furniture as "a complete burlesque of pointed design". But everything else was in Morel and Seddon's distinctive gilt-and-gorgeousness style, including the King's own Bedroom and Closet beyond the White Drawing-room, and the Sitting-room, Boudoir and Bedroom in the south-east tower, later to be occupied by Queen Adelaide and all subsequent queens down to the present day. The King's bath was in an alcove in his Bedroom, covered by a slab of marble (Pl. 73); under William IV or perhaps early in Queen Victoria's reign it was to be concealed in a cupboard (Pl. 74), as were other baths in the guest bedrooms.

It is ironic that George IV, who left his mark on the Castle more than any other monarch, hardly lived there. He moved into the Private Apartments in December 1828; he could not use St George's Hall, the Grand Reception Room and the Waterloo Chamber, because they were not finished in his lifetime. He was back in London in the spring, spent the summer at Royal Lodge, and finally moved back into the Castle in the autumn. He was swollen with drink, dropsy and drugs. He spent more and more time in bed, in a white flannel jacket and cotton nightcap, dozing, drinking and endlessly talking. In the early morning of 26 June, 1830, holding the doctor's hand, he called out: "my dear boy, this is death," and died a few minutes later. *The Times* published a vicious obituary: "There never was an individual less regretted by his fellow-creatures than this deceased king." The Duke of Wellington was fairer: "He was, indeed, the most extraordinary compound of talent, wit, buffoonery, obstinacy, and

65 (above) Queen Victoria and Louis Philippe going into St George's Hall for a banquet on the occasion of his State Visit in October 1844. From the watercolour by Joseph Nash.

66 (right) The Waterloo Chamber, with a dinner to the Emperor of Russia and King of Saxony in progress, 1844.

good feeling — in short a medley of the most opposite qualities, with a great preponderance of good — that I ever saw in any character in my life."

It was left to subsequent monarchs to take advantage of the machinery of royal living which he had set up. From his death up to the present day it has worked so well that it has received only minor modifications. The three big rooms in the State Apartments were finished soon after William IV's accession, and he started using them immediately. He gave regular dinners in St George's Hall on his birthday on 21 August. At the last of these, in 1836, he stood up and made a speech attacking the Duchess of Kent, who was sitting next to him, as "surrounded by evil advisers and ... herself incompetent to act with propriety". But in general his amiable and easy-going style was thought a welcome change from that of his brother. As Charles Greville put it in his diary: "What a *changement de décoration*; no longer George IV, capricious, luxurious and misanthropic, liking nothing but the society of listeners and flatterers ... but a plain, vulgar, hospitable gentleman, opening his doors to all the world."

Life at Windsor was not exciting, however. After dinner the royal family and their guests would settle round two tables in the Crimson Drawing-room. "All the boring she had ever endured before", expostulated Lady Grey to a friend in 1833, "was literally nothing compared with her misery of the two preceding nights. She hoped she never should see a mahogany table again, she was so tired with the one that the Queen, and the King, the Duchess of Gloucester, Princess Augusta, Madame Lieven and herself had sat round for *hours* — the Queen knitting or netting a purse, the King sleeping and occasionally waking for the purpose of saying: 'Exactly so, ma'am!', and then sleeping again."

Within a year of William IV's attack on the Duchess of Kent he was dead, and her daughter had become queen. She was to live at Windsor Castle, on

and off, for nearly sixty-four years, longer than any other monarch. For twenty-one years of this period she was married to Prince Albert. It was at the top, probably, of the Sovereign's Staircase in the Private Apartments that she first saw him when he came to Windsor in 1839, and immediately fell in love with him. It was a few feet away from this staircase that he died, on 14 December, 1861, in the room where George IV and William IV had also died, with his wife by his side. As she wrote in her diary, "I stood up, kissed his dear heavenly forehead and called out in a bitter and agonising cry 'Oh! my dear Darling' and then dropped on my knees in mute, distracted despair."

67 (top left) Queen Victoria walking on the terrace before the east wing on an Open Sunday. From Nash *Windsor Castle*.

68 (bottom left) The Dining-room in the Private Apartments. From Nash *Windsor Castle*.

69 (right) Design by Morel and Seddon for the east wall of the Green Library (later the Green Drawing-room).

The room was kept as a shrine until the Queen's own death (Pl. 75). Its ceiling was painted with angels and stars but otherwise everything was left untouched, the Prince's bed made up every day with the sheets in which he had died, his hat, stick and gloves kept ready for him in the lobby. By the last years of her life the faded blue silk of the wall hangings was so rotten that the Lord Chamberlain's Department fearfully changed it for new silk, faded down to the same colour. She was getting blind, and did not notice.

Prince Albert made reforms in the Household organisation at Windsor, and was the moving spirit behind such architectural changes as took place within the Wyatville framework, including the insertion of a private chapel in the former Band or Orchestra Room (Pl. 76). But while Osborne and Balmoral were his and the Queen's private homes, which they had created together, Windsor was the official residence of the monarch, and the Queen dominated it even during Prince Albert's lifetime; both, however, complained about the bureaucracy of the Department of Woods and Forests, which had to agree and pay for any alterations.

Life as lived by the Queen at Windsor divided into two parts, the everyday life in the Private Apartments and the occasional event in the State Apartments. The Queen occupied the rooms in the South-East (soon known as

the Victoria) Tower. Prince Albert used George IV's rooms, between the Victoria Tower and the White Drawing-room, but seems to have slept with the Queen until his final illness. The nurseries were over the Queen's rooms; and the happy family life of the royal couple (Pl. 77) was much celebrated by her subjects.

The Queen gave private audience to her Prime Ministers and other public figures in the Private Audience Room, a little high-ceilinged room in the south range, close to her tower, which had been decorated for the purpose with some richness under Prince Albert's direction (Pl. 80). She gave unofficial audiences,

70 (left) The Grand Reception Room.

71 (above right) Queen Victoria, the Emperor of Russia, the King of Saxony, Prince Albert and others in the Grand Reception Room on 6 June, 1844. From the water-colour sketch by Joseph Nash.

72 (right) A view at the angle of the Corridor. From Nash *Windsor Castle*.

or saw her family or friends, in her sitting-room, and it was here that she sat at her desk writing her multitudinous, heavily-underlined letters and reading the official papers that came to her in mounting numbers of red boxes, until she was sometimes starting work at six in the morning. In its main lines, and even its main furnishings, it remained as left by George IV, but by the end of her reign it had silted up with ornaments, photographs and personal mementoes — "the orderly confusion of beautiful bric-a-brac", as one description politely put it (Pls. 81-2).

In early years the Queen and Prince Albert breakfasted, and sometimes lunched, in the White Drawing-room (Pl. 79). In later years the function of a breakfast and private dining-room was taken over by what became known as the Oak Breakfast-room, or just the Oak Room, across the corridor and above the Sovereign's Entrance. This was used more and more in the Queen's last years (Pl. 83).

But the regular formal event in the Private Apartments, when the Queen had guests, was dinner in the gothic Dining-room (Pl. 68) beyond the Crimson Drawing-room. This followed a pattern which varied comparatively little during the reign, and is still recognisably the one observed today. There were usually around fifteen to twenty-five at dinner, a mixture of Household, family,

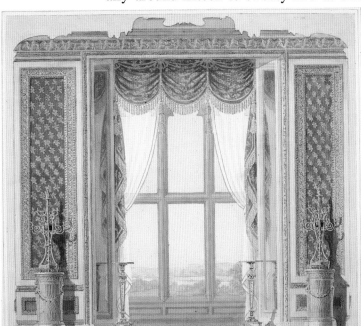

and friends staying for several days, and of members of the Cabinet, ambassadors, or people (varying from Alfred Tennyson to Lord Kitchener) whom the Queen wished to see, and who came for dinner and stayed the night.

Guests assembled in the Crimson Drawing-room (Pl. 85) or, later in the reign, in the Corridor (Pl. 84) between 8.30 and 8.45 p.m. ("I wondered", the American Consuelo, Duchess of Marlborough recalls, "why, with all the rooms the Castle possessed, we should be confined to

73 (top left) Design by Morel and Seddon for the bath in King George IV's bedroom. The bath is now in the Victoria and Albert Museum.

74 (bottom left) Another design by Morel and Seddon for the room which later became the Queen's living room.

75 (above) The Blue Room, where Prince Albert died, from a watercolour made in about 1865 by William Coden. George IV and William IV died in the same room.

this small passage.") They waited for the Queen to come out of her rooms and along the Corridor, when everyone followed her into dinner. After dinner she and the ladies left first, but the men were only allowed to stay five minutes or so. Sometimes she returned almost immediately to her own room, stopping on her way to talk to the guests individually in the Corridor, but on most evenings she went with them into one of the drawing-rooms. Sometimes there was a musical evening, at which famous musicians or singers like Adelina Patti or Paderewski would perform. Sometimes a Maid of Honour would be asked to sing or play. In early years a whist table would be set up for the Duchess of Kent, and the remainder would sit around a round table with the Queen, as in William IV's day, playing spillikins or round games, or watching Prince Albert's card tricks. A regular pattern in later years was for the ladies to be invited one by one to sit by her (never initiating a subject, which was against protocol), while the remainder were free to perambulate the rooms standing. According to one account, "it is the rule not to raise the voice when speaking, and loud laughter is considered a gross breach of courtly manners."

The Queen usually retired to her rooms at about eleven o'clock. The ladies then also went to their rooms, but the men, if they felt like it, could take a long walk to the billiard room, on the ground floor beyond St George's Hall. This was the only room where they were allowed to smoke. Baron d'Estournelle de Constant once left it very late at night, could not find his way past St George's Hall and was reduced to sleeping on a sofa in the Grand Reception Room.

76 (above) The Private Chapel. Designed by Edward Blore and installed in 1842 in the space formerly used by the Royal Band. This was the room in which the fire started in 1992.

77 (right) Queen Victoria and Prince Albert watching their children from the window of the Queen's Sitting-room. From a lithograph of 1850.

Victoria hated gaslight. By 1846 gas had penetrated to the courts and outer extremities at Windsor, but up till the end of her reign all the Private Apartments, including the big rooms, were lit by candlelight, although there were paraffin lamps on the staircases leading up to them. (At the end of the reign, when the Queen made a good deal of use of an invalid chair, a lift for her was installed by the Sovereign's Staircase, "well arranged in oak, gold, and crimson upholstery"). She also intensely disliked the smell of coal, and only beech logs were allowed to burn in the grates of the private apartments. Thermometers, set in ivory obelisks of identical design, stood on every chimneypiece to regulate the room to an identical temperature. It was not a high one, for the Queen had a passion for fresh air; on cold winter days she would walk up and down the Corridor to keep warm (there was no central heating). On warmer days she often sat in the Corridor. It was also used for games by the royal children and their friends (mostly children of members of the Household); it was, one of them later recalled, "a grand place for races".

The Queen had a lively interest in what was going on around her, and a feeling heart. She could inspire great devotion as a result; but she also had an abundant sense of her position and dignity as Queen. Royal protocol required that no commoner sat in the presence of the monarch, except at his or her request; and there was a great deal of standing at Windsor. Life there was never relaxed, and grew stiffer and sadder after the Prince Consort's death. As early as 1838 Charles Greville commented: "the Court is not gay, but it is perhaps impossible that any Court should be gay where there is no social equality; where some ceremony, and a continual air of deference and respect must be observed, there can be no ease, and without ease there can be no real pleasure ...very little is done in common, and in this respect Windsor is totally unlike

any other place. There is none of the sociability which makes the agreeableness of an English country house; there is no room in which the guests assemble, sit, lounge, and talk as they please and when they please; there is a billiard table, but in such a remote corner of the Castle that it might as well be in the town of Windsor; and there is a library well stocked with books, but hardly accessible, imperfectly warmed, and only tenanted by the librarian; it is a mere library too, unfurnished, and offering none of the comforts and luxuries of a hospitable room." In her later years guests found their visits to a castle so totally dominated by one tiny black-clad figure an interesting but daunting experience.

The Queen's part of the Castle could hold considerable numbers of people, but a big event would stretch it beyond capacity. For the christening of the Prince of Wales, for instance, on 25 January, 1842, one hundred and sixteen people were accommodated. Sixty-one of these slept in the Upper Ward, and ten in the Round Tower, which Wyatville had linked by a staircase to the Corridor, to provide for this kind of situation. The rest were dispersed in grace-and-favour apartments all over the Castle, or down in the Home Park at Frogmore Lodge. The guests included the King of Prussia, godfather and principal guest, numerous royal dukes, princes and princesses, half-a-dozen ambassadors and most of the Cabinet.

78 (left) Some of Queen Victoria's grand-children photographed in July 1890, in a donkey carriage in the Home Park before the east front of the Upper Ward.

79 (above) The White Drawing-room, with Queen Victoria and Prince Albert at break-fast or luncheon. From Nash *Windsor Castle*.

80 (right) The Private Audience Chamber.

The King of Prussia was put up in the portion of the State Apartments which had been the King's and Queen's Privy Lodgings under Charles II. These rooms had been left in something of a limbo by Wyatville's alterations, since the official Drawing-rooms for which he had earmarked them seldom if ever took place at Windsor. State visits by royalty gave them, and indeed the whole Castle, a new function (Pls. 65-6, 71, 86).

Such visits were a new development. In earlier centuries kings and queens had not left their kingdoms, except in war, and not entertained other kings and queens except as prisoners or by accident. Their palaces had no accommodation for them. When King Philip of Castile took refuge in England from a storm in 1505, and was put up for a few nights at Windsor Castle, Henry VII had to give up his own lodgings to him.

81 (above) The Queen's Sitting-room. From Nash *Windsor Castle*.

82 (right) Queen Victoria and Beatrice, Princess Henry of Battenberg, in the Queen's Sitting-room, 1895.

It may have been the French Revolution and the subsequent wars and displacements which encouraged royalty to become more mobile. The first proper state visits to England were those of the Emperor of Russia and King of Saxony to London in 1814; the Emperor of Russia had been offered the Duke of Cumberland's apartments in St James's Palace, for lack of anything better, and had gone off in a huff to a hotel. But Windsor Castle was an ideal venue in which to entertain and impress visiting royalty, and state visits to it became a feature of Victoria's and all subsequent reigns.

83 (left) Queen
Victoria, Prince
and Princess
Henry of
Battenberg and
their children
lunching in the
Oak Room, 1895.

84 (above)
Another view in
the Corridor.
From Nash
Windsor Castle.

Visits followed a similar pattern. Observing royal protocol, the Queen
came down to the State Entrance to welcome a monarch, but for other ranks of
royalty she stood at the top of the Staircase and they came up to her. The stairs
were lined with Yeomen of the Guard or soldiers of the Household Cavalry, in
full rig. "Are they real?" asked the son of the Emir of Afghanistan in 1895, and
stroked one of them, to make sure. The royal visitor would then be conducted
by the Queen to the Garter Throne-room and introduced to her family. It was in
this room, but not on the occasion of a full state visit, that the Queen sat on her
throne to receive members of a deputation from Siam in 1858 (Pl. 87). They
insisted on following Siamese protocol and approaching her on all fours.
"Really, it was most difficult to keep one's countenance," wrote the Queen.

The Emperor of Russia and the King of Saxony came in 1844, Louis-
Philippe and his queen later in the same year, Napoleon III and the Empress
Eugénie in 1855. For the latter visit a late-eighteenth century French bed was
set up in the former King's State Bedchamber, where it still is (Pl. 88). It was
given new hangings in the Napoleonic colours, decorated with the monograms

of Emperor and Empress. On the first evening there was a State Ball, with supper in St George's Hall, and dancing in the Waterloo Chamber, tactfully referred to as the Music Room for the duration of the visit. The Queen danced with the Emperor, and wrote in her diary, in which there was no need for tact, "Really to think that I, the grand-daughter of George III, should dance with the Emperor Napoleon, nephew to our great enemy, now my nearest and most intimate ally, in the Waterloo Room too — and this ally, only six years ago, an exile, poor, comparatively little known, living in this country, seems incredible."

The Queen gave other balls in the State Apartments, and small dances from time to time in the Crimson Drawing-room. After the Prince Consort's death she never danced, attended a dance or gave one. For some years entertaining of all kinds at the Castle was very muted. Even the Prince of Wales's wedding in St George's Chapel, on 10 March, 1863, was played down. Princess Alexandra's parents were installed in the State Apartments, there were processions to and from the Chapel and a splendid ceremony. But the Queen took no part in the processions, and watched the ceremony from up in the Royal Closet, a solitary figure in black. She made her way to it privately, by way of the North Terrace, the Deanery and a board-walk laid on the Dean's Cloister roof; this still exists. There was no banquet in St George's Hall, only a family dinner in the private Dining-room, which the Queen did not attend.

But big functions, including State Visits, began again in the last decades of her reign, starting with the visit of the Shah of Persia in 1873. State Visits now usually involved dinner in St George's Hall, followed by some kind of musical event in the Waterloo Chamber, but never a ball. When the Kaiser came in 1895 one of his German orderlies had spent the night sleeping on a mat outside his bedroom door, in a manner reminiscent of the Gentlemen and Grooms in the days of Charles II.

85 (left) The Crimson Drawing-room.

86 (above) The Upper Ward by moonlight, with a royal visitor arriving. From Nash *Windsor Castle*.

81

87 (above) A
deputation from
Siam approaches
Queen Victoria
in the Garter
Throne-room,
1858.

88 (right) The
King's Bedroom
in the State
Apartments, with
the bed installed
in it for the visit
of the Emperor
Napoleon III and
the Empress
Eugénie in 1855.

The Queen had always adored entertainment of all kinds. In the Prince Consort's day London companies regularly brought down plays from the West End and put them on in the "Rubens Room" or King's Drawing-room in the State Apartments. The entertainment commanded by or put on for her at Windsor from about 1875 onwards included conjuring shows, a circus in the Riding School, Buffalo Bill's Wild West Show in the East Garden, "animated pictures" ("a very wonderful process, representing people, their movements and actions, as if they were alive", wrote the Queen), plays or skits mounted by the family and members of the Household, numerous concerts and, above all, operas.

The operas were a feature of her last years. They were put on by the best available companies from London, on a stage constructed in the Waterloo Chamber (Pl. 89). In all, nine operas were mounted between 1893 and 1900, including, on one gruelling evening, both *Carmen* and *Cavaleria Rusticana*. The evenings must have been disconcerting for the performers, for the Queen never applauded, and of course no-one else could applaud either. But after the opera was over the leading members of the caste were invited to meet the Queen in one of the drawing-rooms, and presented with a memento: cuff-links or pins for the men, brooches for the women, sometimes an ornamental baton for the conductor, all with the Queen's monogram on them.

One of the most successful evenings in the Waterloo Chamber was on 17

May, 1898, when Johann Strauss brought his orchestra down to Windsor; he conducted "playing on a miniature violin with his back to the orchestra, being too gallant to turn his back on the Queen". She loved the performance and — a great rarity for her — asked for two encores, including one of the "Blue Danube".

The description is by A.G. Seymour, who worked in the Lord

89 (above) The Waterloo Chamber arranged for a performance of *Romeo and Juliet* on 27 June, 1898.

90 (top right) King Edward VII's bathroom in the Private Apartments.

91 (bottom right) The Queen's Sitting-room in the time of Queen Alexandra.

Chamberlain's office at Windsor, and was closely involved in the organisation of these events. He goes on to describe the changes in Edward VII's day: no more operas, instead successful West-End plays or shows, or Souza's Military Band, and the King vigorously leading the applause. It was part of a new look for the Castle: the State Apartments completely re-arranged, the old Queen's Scottish and Indian servants got rid of, up-to-date bathrooms (Pl. 90), the Prince Consort's bedroom cleared out and re-decorated as the King's study. Queen Alexandra moved into the Victoria Tower and filled the sitting-room with her own Edwardian clutter (Pl. 91). But the new king came to Windsor much less often than his mother, often for no more than a State Visit in November and a visit for Ascot in the Summer.

Seymour, looking back after retirement, contrasted "the dignified aloofness of Her Majesty, the bright smiling presence of Queen Alexandra, and the business-like bearing of Queen Mary". Queen Mary's hobby was re-arranging rooms, to the despair of her staff. Entertainments in the Waterloo Chamber

under King George V were confined to cinema shows. A later episode in the room's history came during the war, when a pantomime was put on by royal family and Household for three consecutive years at Christmas, with the glowing and excited Princess Elizabeth and Princess Margaret Rose in the lead roles (Pl. 94). The Lawrences had been removed for safety, and the empty spaces they had filled in the panelling were decorated by an art-student with brightly-coloured paintings of pantomime characters. These were revealed when the paintings

93 (right) The Queen's Sitting-room in the time of Queen Elizabeth the Queen Mother.

were removed again during the recent fire, with bizarre effect in so grand and enormous a room.

In recent years, up till the 1992 fire, the Waterloo Chamber was used for the annual Garter lunch, for concerts in the Autumn Windsor Festival, and for plays, revues, performances of Gilbert and Sullivan, and Christmas concerts. State banquets were still being held in St George's Hall. The big rooms in the Private Apartments were being used much as in Queen Victoria's day. The

Queen occupies the Victoria Tower, like her mother, grandmother, and great-grandmother before her (Pls. 81-2, 91-3). The Duke of Edinburgh uses King Edward VII's study; children's bicycles and go-karts are lined up by the Sovereign's Entrance; there is a swimming-pool in the orangery; and the royal corgis pad up and down the Corridor.

94 (above) The Princesses Elizabeth and Margaret Rose dressed for a pantomime in the Waterloo Chamber.
95 (right) The statue of Charles II at the foot of the Round Tower. It was the gift of Tobias Rustat, Yeoman of the Robes and Page of the Backstairs to Charles II.

4 Royal Servants

Royal life at Windsor was only made possible by great numbers of servants. Royalty was the glittering tip of an iceberg resting on the cumbrous mass of the Royal Household, much of it operating under the social equivalent of the water level. Literally hundreds of people were, and though in reducing numbers, still are involved, and a labyrinth of rooms, upstairs, downstairs and in towers and corners all over the Castle, grew up to accommodate them. These rooms are never seen by the general public, but they include some of the most ancient and interesting rooms at Windsor.

The history of the Royal Household is an extremely complicated one, but it helps to understand it if one grasps a few basic facts. Each room in the Royal Lodgings, upstairs and downstairs, originally had its own group of servants, and as new rooms appeared new servants appeared with them. The person of the monarch could originally only be served by people of title, for the closest and most personal services, and by gentlemen and ladies, for other kinds of attendance (Pl. 96). Over the centuries services to the body of the monarch were gradually handed over from the upper to the middle and lower classes. Changing uses of rooms and changing technologies created new servants, and made old ones less important or completely unnecessary.

Usually this meant that they continued to draw their wages, with nothing or very little to do. At intervals, every few decades, the waste and expense which this involved would lead to a move for economy and reform of the Household, sometimes originating from the monarch or the upper members of the Household, sometimes as a response to public outcry; then Masters of the Royal Tennis Court, where no tennis had been played for centuries, Royal Furriers, who supplied no furs, and Gentlemen Usher Quarterly Waiters, who no longer ushered or waited, would cease to exist, or at least cease to draw their perquisites or comfortable salaries.

What were to remain the main divisions of the Household until comparatively recent years had appeared at least by the time of King Stephen, in the twelfth century. It corresponded to the two main rooms of the Royal Lodgings of those days, the Hall and the Chamber. The Hall was under the charge of a steward, the Chamber of a chamberlain. The two men developed into the Lord Chamberlain and the Lord Steward of the Household, two great and powerful officers of state dividing the rule of the Household between them: roughly speaking, the Lord Chamberlain was responsible for life above stairs, the Lord Steward for life below them. In the fourteenth century a third great officer appeared, in the person of the Master of the Horse, in charge of the great numbers of horses required for the daily use of the Household and its periodical moves from place to place.

Between the twelfth and the sixteenth centuries one can watch the Household expand. In the Lord Chamberlain's realm, for instance, as the Great Chamber spawned the Privy Chamber, the Privy Chamber spawned the Bedchamber and the royal bed moved from one to the other, new officers were created or old ones upped in importance. One of the most curious developments was the rise of the Groom of the Stole. The origins of this, for a time, extremely important officer are wrapped in some obscurity, but what seems to have happened was this. When the royal bed moved out of the Privy Chamber into a separate Bedchamber in the fifteenth century, the office of a minor royal servant, the Groom of the Stool or Stole, was increased in importance. His sphere had previously been the king's stool, that is to say, he looked after the king's garderobe or privy. When promoted, this official kept his old title, but by the seventeenth century, if not before, he had become a power in the Household, usually an earl, in charge of the king's two Bedchambers, his Closet and his Backstairs, of the Gentlemen (all lords, in fact) and Grooms of the Bedchamber, and the Pages of the Backstairs, and ruling over his little province, which was politically as well as socially of the greatest importance, in complete independence of the Lord Chamberlain. So grand a person did not like to be reminded of the ignoble origins of his office; and so historians obligingly told him that the 'stole' was originally part of the royal robes, of which that particular groom had had charge. His office and realm survived until both were abolished on or soon after the accession of Queen Victoria.

Another change in Household life at Windsor is marked by the change in

THE SERVANTS' HALL.

Central Panel. Chimney-piece.

STEWARD'S ROOM.

97 (top) The Servants' Hall. From a drawing by C.A. Buckler, *c.* 1860. The room forms a major part of the mid-fourteenth century undercroft below St George's Hall.

98 (above) The Steward's Room. From a drawing by C.A. Buckler. Its vaulting dates from the thirteenth century.

99 (right) The corridor by the Steward's Room. It was added alongside it in the mid-fourteenth century to get the requisite width to support the southern end of St George's Hall.

100 (below) The Great Kitchen in the early nine-teenth century. From Pyne *Royal Residences*.

name of the hall, from "Great Hall" or "King's Great Hall" in medieval and Tudor days to "St George's Hall".The first known use of the last term is in a survey of 1629. The change of name must reflect a change of function, from the room where the greater part of the Household regularly ate (as laid down in detail, for instance, in regulations for the Household of Edward IV) but which was also used for the annual Garter Feast, to a purely ceremonial hall, used only for Garter Feasts and other events of the same nature.

The move out of the hall had in fact start-ed in the sixteenth century. Members of the Household at all levels increasingly either drew board wages, or had food from the kitchens sent to eating-rooms or lodgings

scattered over the Castle. It was not perhaps until the early nineteenth century that the non-gentry part of the Household was finally consolidated in the undercroft below St George's Hall. As their Servants' Hall (Pl. 97) the lower servants moved into the major part of a magnificent rib-vaulted room divided down its axis by a row of columns, a setting rather more impressive and a great deal solider than the plaster Gothic of Wyatville's hall where monarchs were banqueting above them.

This room dated from the mid-fourteenth century, and was probably built as the royal wine or beer-cellar. Adjoining it to the south a smaller and narrower vaulted room of the thirteenth century became the Steward's Room (Pl. 98), for the upper servants. The room now contains a fine chimneypiece decorated with the rose of Edward IV. This is not in its original position, however, and may be a last precious survival from the big rooms of the medieval King's Lodgings.

On its own court beyond these and other vaulted rooms was, and still is (though the court has been filled in) the Great Kitchen (Pl. 100). It and the peripheral rooms were ruled over by the Clerk of the Kitchen, one of the most important of the officials in the Lord Steward's department. The aquatint in Pyne's *Royal Residences* and the watercolour on which it is based show this splendid room as it was in 1819. It looked then, and was still used, much as in the Middle Ages. Most of the cooking was done by boiling or roasting at huge open fires. The room was top-lit from a medieval timber roof, which had been sealed off with a plaster cove at some later date; by Pyne's time the cove had

101 (above) Yeomen of the Guard in attendance in the King's Guard-room. Detail from the illustration in Pyne *Royal Residences*.

102 (right) Bridget Holmes, aged ninety-six, painted by John Riley in 1686. She had been in service at Windsor since the reign of Charles I.

BRIDGET. HOLMES)
ETA: SUÆ: 96 A:D: 1686

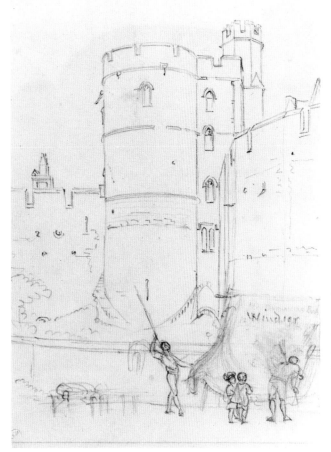

been painted to imitate the stonework of the walls. An adjacent kitchen had been added in the late seventeenth century, perhaps as a Privy Kitchen for the royal meals. But during much of the nineteenth century the Great Kitchen served all levels of the Household, from the king or queen downwards.

In and around the Kitchen was a maze of other rooms occupying related functions, all under the ultimate rule of the Lord Steward, paid and, if needs be, disciplined by his Board of Green Cloth, which occupied the north-east tower of the Upper Ward. Some idea of their function can be gathered by the list of individuals of departments given the annual presents known as "rewards" on New Year's Day, 1611: the Cellar, the Buttery (for beer), the Pantry (for bread), the Woodyard, the children of the Kitchen, the turnbroaches (who turned the spits), the scourbroaches (who cleaned the Kitchen), the blower (did he light the fire?), the Larders, the Pastry, the Ewery (in charge of linen), the Scalding-house, the Boiling-house, the Scullery, the Poultry, the Chandry (for candles), the Spicery, the Confectionery, the Saucery, the porters, the glasser, the locksmith, the sweeper, the woodbearer, the Timber-yard.

Into this teeming below-stairs world there marched, every dinner and supper time, the Yeomen of the Guard or Beefeaters, wearing the picturesque uniform which dated from their founding by Henry VII. The Yeomen (Pl. 101) acted as a link between the world of the Lord Steward and that of the Lord Chamberlain. For most of the day and night, they stood or sat around in the Guard-chamber (forty in the daytime, and twenty at night, in the eighteenth century); they accompanied the monarch in processions; but to these functions, more ones of status than security, they added the more practical one of bringing the king's food up from the Kitchen to his Lodgings whenever he was in residence.

It would have been inconceivable, however, for mere Yeomen to have served the monarch. If the latter was eating in the Presence Chamber, they handed the dishes over to the Gentlemen Usher Daily and Quarterly Waiters attached to that room; the latter then served it to the monarch, under the direction of an important officer known as the Sewer. If the monarch was eating in the Privy Chamber, or anywhere else in the Privy Apartments, a curious procedure was gone through, at least in the reign of Elizabeth. The meal was served with great ceremony to the royal table in the Presence Chamber, as if

103 (above) Carpet-beating below the Stone Tower in the Middle Ward. From the drawing by Paul Sandby. Perhaps carried out under the Lady Housekeeper, one of the few resident officers left at Windsor Castle before George III moved back there.

the Queen were sitting there; the Gentleman Usher and Daily Waiter of the Privy Chamber then appeared from next door and carried the food through to be eaten, with much less ceremony, by the Queen.

The Privy Apartments were kept clean by Yeomen of the Chamber, but all the other servants in them were at least gentlemen and ladies, and a good many were lords. Something has been said about this in the previous chapter, but it is worth having a look at the junior officers of the department, the Pages of the Backstairs, for they were an interesting example of how being in on the action could give a servant influence and power.

Through almost all Charles II's reign the senior Page was William Chiffinch. He also served as keeper of the King's Closet, and had his own rooms on the ground floor off the approach to the Backstairs. He was the King's most confidential servant. He controlled who came in and out by the Backstairs, and looked after the King's secret money affairs. The King enjoyed passing the evening with his drinking companions in Chiffinch's own room; there too the genial Page of the Backstairs used to invite people in, get them drunk and "so fished out many secrets and discovered men's characters, which the King could never have obtained the knowledge of by any other means". He left a comfortable fortune, and married his daughter to the future Earl of Jersey.

The statue of Charles II which now stands at the foot of the Round Tower (Pl. 95) was the gift of Tobias Rustat, Yeoman of the Robes and one of his Pages of the Backstairs. It is probably a junior Page who holds back the curtain in the portrait by John Riley of Bridget Holmes, painted in 1686 (Pl. 102). This "necessary woman" at the Castle is painted with all the pomp of a Field Marshal, but wearing an apron and holding a broom instead of a baton. So grand a painting is probably less a tribute to the importance of a necessary woman than to her age and service: she had started her service under Charles I and was ninety-six when Riley painted her (she was to live to one hundred). But her actual existence is significant of the arrival of women in the Royal Household. Up till the seventeenth century, apart from the Queen's Maids and Ladies, the Royal Household was almost exclusively male, like other big households of the time. The Kitchen was entirely made up of men; it was Yeomen of the Chamber, not chambermaids, who cleaned out the Privy Lodgings. Women cleaners and bedmakers arrived in the seventeenth century and they, and later a Housekeeper to run them, were to become increasingly important.

Another significant change is heralded by an entry in a letter from Lord Clarendon, written in 1688. He remarks in passing that when he waited on Princess Anne (the future Queen) in her Bedchamber, he found "one of her dressers with her". Here, but in the context of a royal princess only, is the appearance of an attendant not of gentle birth, helping to dress her. When she became Queen, however, dressers disappeared or melted into the background, to judge by the information given to Lady Suffolk by Mrs Masham, who had

been Woman of the Bedchamber to the Queen (and in that position had acquired political influence rather greater than that of William Chiffinch). The Bedchamber Woman gave the Queen's shift to the Bedchamber Lady, and the latter put it on. When the Queen washed her hands, the Page of the Backstairs brought in the basin and ewer and the Bedchamber Woman, kneeling, poured it over the Queen's hands while the Bedchamber Lady looked on. "The Bedchamber-Woman pulled on the Queen's gloves, when she could not do it herself. The Page of the Backstairs was called in to put on the Queen's shoes."

Customs began to change under George III. By at least the middle of his reign the King was dressing himself when he got up, and the Groom of the Stole and Lord of the Bedchamber were only in attendance to help him put on ceremonial dress for his afternoon levée. The Queen still had her Ladies and Women of the Bedchamber, but in the 1780s her actual dressing and undressing was carried out by Mrs Schwellenberg, her Keeper of the Robes, Fanny Burney, Assistant Keeper, and Mrs Thielcke, her Wardrobe Woman, who all came from a middle- rather than upper-class background; the fact that Fanny Burney's talents had already made her a best-selling novelist had nothing to do with her appointment, but enabled her to give some lively descriptions of her experiences at the Queen's Lodge at Windsor and elsewhere, under the kindly Queen and bad-tempered Mrs Schwellenberg. Fanny and Mrs Schwellenberg helped the Queen dress and undress in her Dressing-room but did not go into her Bedchamber, except in emergencies; she was actually put to bed by Mrs Thielcke. The King and Queen still had their meals served to them by lords and ladies, however; and anyone leaving a room when they were in it still had to go out backwards.

Under George III Equerries begin to come into prominence. They were originally officers attached to the Stable (the word originates from the French *écuyer,* horse-rider, and *écurie,* stable), responsible for breaking-in the king's horses and preparing them for him to ride. They now began to develop into something closer to ADCs, who not only went out riding with the king, but helped in organizing his inside and outside engagements.

104 (above) Queen Victoria's Indian servant and secretary, Hafiz Abdul Karim, known as the Munshi.

105 (right) Queen Victoria's dresser, Annie McDonald, from a water-colour by the Queen.

98

One last vignette from the recollections of Charles Knight. At card or other parties given in the Royal Lodgings in the Castle, in the time of George III, the candles were all blown out the moment the evening was considered to have ended, leaving the guests to fumble out in the dark. This was not because of royal meanness, as was sometimes alleged. The explanation was simple: unfinished candles were the perquisites of the relevant Household officers, who could take them off and sell them. No candle was ever lit a second time. It was not surprising that in 1812 the House of Commons was told that the bill for wax candles at Windsor came to ten thousand pounds a year.

QUEEN VICTORIA.

George III was aware of this but believed in tradition, and had a kindly nature. One day, having left his Library for the evening he unexpectedly returned to it from the Drawing-room, and found the candles still burning. He went back to the Drawing-room and told the relevant Page: "Clarke, Clarke, you should mind your perquisites. *I* blew out the candles."

Thirty or forty years later Prince Albert who, though by no means averse to tradition, had a passionate belief in efficiency and rational organisation, got to grips with the Royal Household and did his best to make it work. By the 1840s the system had grown increasingly political; all the more senior members of the Household, male and female, changed with each change of government; it was remarked in 1837 that "a Conservative cat was not so much as permitted even to mew within the precincts of the Queen's palaces". Five Lord Chamberlains between 1830 and 1842 did not make for efficiency. Moreover the demarcation of authority between the spheres of Lord Chamberlain, Lord Steward and Master of the Horse was by no means clear. The footmen, for instance, had originally been attached to the Stables, employed to run alongside the carriages, and were under the command of the Master of the Horse; by the nineteenth century half of them had come to wait at table and perform other services inside the Castle, but the Master of the Horse still controlled them. The story is well known of how the Queen asked the servants in attendance

why she had no fire and was told that they were in the Lord Steward's department, which was responsible for laying it, but that it was the Lord Chamberlain's
department which lit it.

The Lord Chamberlain and Lord Steward were powerful officers, jealous
of their realms, and Prince Albert had to work by persuasion and representation. His main concern was to make a clear and sensible division of responsi-
bilities, and his main achievement to increase the role of the Master of the
Household. This officer had been created in the sixteenth century as the deputy
to the Lord Steward, but his duties were far from clear. He was now made the
resident non-political deputy of all three major officers, the Lord Chamberlain,
the Lord Steward and the Master of the Horse, in command of the personnel of
their departments who worked inside the royal palaces. Another innovation
inspired by Prince Albert was the creation of a separate Royal Laundry at Kew,
serving both Windsor Castle and Buckingham Palace. These and other changes
made the Household more efficient, and possibly cheaper; but towards the end
of the reign, its expense and inefficiency were again causing concern.

Throughout the reign of Queen Victoria the Royal Household was still
firmly divided, as it always had been, into two layers — one of gentlemen and
ladies, and the other of non-gentle birth, but the upper layer was no longer
performing any bodily services to the monarch. Her Mistress of the Robes and
Ladies of the Bedchamber seldom if ever penetrated into her bedroom, which
was the province of her dressers and ladies' maids. The former (Pl. 105) came
from what might be described as good governess stock. A Page of the
Backstairs sat in permanent attendance in the lobby outside the bedroom, but,
although a person of importance in the running of the Castle, he was no longer

106 (left) The
Equerries' Room
in the 1930s.

107 (above) A
Household group
in about 1890.
Seated, left to
right: Dr James
Reid, Sir Henry
Ponsonby, the
Queen's Private
Secretary, and
Marie Adeane,
Maid of Honour;
on ground: Alick
Yorke, Groom in
Waiting and
Major Arthur
Bigge, Equerry
and Assistant
Private
Secretary.

of gentle birth, but a servant who had worked his way up from being a footman; unlike Will Chiffinch, his daughter was unlikely to marry an earl.

The Lords and Grooms in waiting no longer waited on the Queen, as in the days of George III, but sat at dinner with her and were waited on by Pages of the Presence and footmen, by the Groom and Yeomen of the Cellars (to pour out the drink), and in her last years by stately and silent Indian servants (Pl. 83), who had their own separate quarters and separate food in the Castle. The Clerk of the Kitchen was in attendance to supervise the whole operation. One of the Indian servants was promoted as the Queen's Munshi (Hindu for teacher), and later as her "Indian secretary", and was to be much criticised by the Household, other members of the royal family and the Government for his undue influence and supposed disloyalty (Pl. 104). In general, the Queen's relationships with her upper Household tended to be stiff, and she often got on better with people of servant class, the best-known of whom was John Brown, the Scottish ghillie promoted to be her personal attendant.

The changing nature of the upper Household (which tended and still tends to attract the term "Household" to itself alone) meant that its numbers were greatly reduced from the serried ranks of Lords, Gentlemen, Ladies and Maids who were in attendance in Stuart or early Hanoverian days. And of the total only a small proportion were "in waiting" at any one time. The Queen had, for instance, eight Maids of Honour, but they were in waiting two at a time (each for three one-month periods) along with one of the eight Ladies of the Bedchamber, a permanent Woman of the Bedchamber, who was effectively her personal secretary, one permanent Lord in waiting, one of the eight Equerries and one of the eight Grooms in waiting.

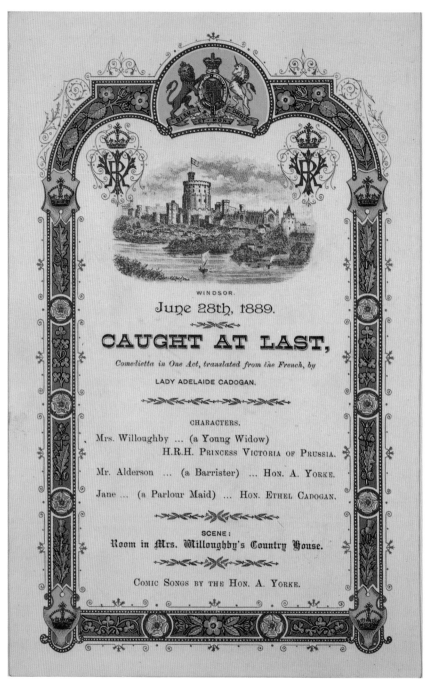

WINDSOR.

June 28th, 1889.

CAUGHT AT LAST,

Comedietta in One Act, translated from the French, by

LADY ADELAIDE CADOGAN.

CHARACTERS.

Mrs. Willoughby ... (a Young Widow)
H.R.H. Princess Victoria of Prussia.

Mr. Alderson ... (a Barrister) ... Hon. A. Yorke.

Jane ... (a Parlour Maid) ... Hon. Ethel Cadogan.

SCENE:
Room in Mrs. Willoughby's Country House.

Comic Songs by the Hon. A. Yorke.

The Maids of Honour were appointed as the result of a personal invitation from the Queen and were usually related to someone who was in, or had been in, the Royal Household. They were required by her to be of gentle birth, unmarried and with no known plans to marry, able to speak French, sing, play the piano, write in a clear but feminine hand and, in the Queen's earlier years, ride. They lived at the extreme end of the Corridor, in what was known as the Devil's Tower; they had their own bedrooms and common sitting-room, into which no man was allowed. One of them dined with the Queen each evening, along with the Lady, Lord and Groom in waiting and one of the Equerries; in-

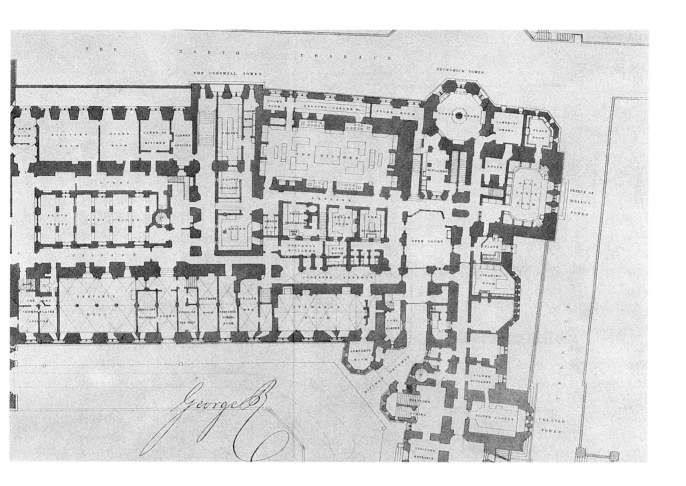

deed, one of the main functions of this part of the Household was now to look after and entertain the Queen and her guests at dinner and afterwards. The Maids and Lady of the Bedchamber were also in attendance on the Queen from time to time during the day, as and when she wanted them; but in terms of looking after her person their services were more or less limited to pinning on her shawl, like Alice on to the White Queen.

108 (left) One of many entertainments put on by members of the royal family and Household. The programme uses a Windsor menu card.

The Maids and Ladies lunched with the Lord in waiting, originally in a charming octagonal room in the Brunswick Tower, but later in the Private Dining-room. The Equerries breakfasted and lunched in their own room, next to their sitting-room on the ground floor (Pl. 106), along with the Queen's Private Secretary, Master of the Household, Groom in Waiting and, in the Queen's later years, the Resident Physician, Sir James Reid. A doctor was still considered not quite a gentleman in Court circles, and it was Reid's humour, liveliness and charm that elevated him to eating with the Household and finally to marriage with one of the Maids of Honour, Susan Baring. This was too much for the Queen, however (she hated her Maids marrying anyway), and she sulked for three days, but finally relented and laughed when Reid promised "not to do it again". All the Household, male and female, who were not dining with the Queen, dined together.

109 (above) The kitchens and offices as they were re-organised by Jeffry Wyatville. Detail from the plan in J. Ashton *Illustrations of Windsor Castle* (1841).

The Household, in the limited sense of the word, formed a curious little

society on its own, set apart from the rest of the world (as is still the case with courtiers today) by the constant need to be tactful and discreet. But there was a good deal of variety (and not a little tension) under the uniformity. The Court joker for many years was Alick Yorke, first an Equerry and later a Groom in waiting, a plump, benign and much-loved pansy who was the leading spirit in the numerous amateur theatricals (Pl. 108) in which Household and royal family took part. He excelled in comic songs and imitations — one of which produced the Queen's famous response "We are not amused".

Social lines were hard and fast at Windsor. Royalty and upper Household could act and sing comic songs together, but it would have been inconceivable for any of the denizens of the Steward's Room to have taken part with them, though they lived and ate in some state in their vaulted Hall, looked after by the Yeoman of the Steward's Room and his five assistants. They were the aristocrats of the warren of service rooms on the ground floor below the State Apartments (Pl. 109). Their room was presided over by the Clerk of the Kitchen,

110 (above) The Great Kitchen in 1878.

111 (right) The Great Kitchen as photographed shortly before the fire in 1992.

and amongst those eating there were his Assistant Clerks, the House-keeper, the Queen's dressers and ladies' maids, the Gentlemen and Yeomen of the Wine Cellar, the Yeoman Confectioner, the Pastry Cook, the First and Second Table-deckers, the Pages, the Queen's Messengers and the valets of visitors, but not those of the male members of the upper Household, who had to eat in the Servants' Hall.

Professionalising the Housekeeper was one of Prince Albert's reforms. At Victoria's accession, Windsor was under the charge of Lady Mary Fox, the illegitimate daughter of William IV. She had the title of Lady Housekeeper, lived in some style in the Norman Tower (where the Governor of Windsor Castle lives today), and had a salary of three hundred and twenty pounds a year and perquisites said to amount to between one thousand two hundred and one thousand five

hundred pounds, derived from fees paid by visitors to the State Apartments. She employed a deputy to do the actual work of a housekeeper. She was "induced to retire" in 1845, and the deputy took over. The latter had a salary of three hundred pounds and no perquisites, and presided over about forty house-maids when the Court was at Windsor.

The Table-deckers were in charge of laying and arranging the royal tables. There were five in all, including a "wax-fitter", who presumably put up the candles. Linen was looked after by the Yeoman of the Ewery and his two female assistants, all eating in the Servants' Hall, as did the three Yeomen of the Pantry and their seven burly helpers. The gold and silver plate which they looked after was said, even in the 1890s, to be worth three million pounds. It was kept in two vaulted and iron-doored Plate Pantries, one for silver and one for gold, with rooms for cleaning adjacent. Periodically large quantities of it

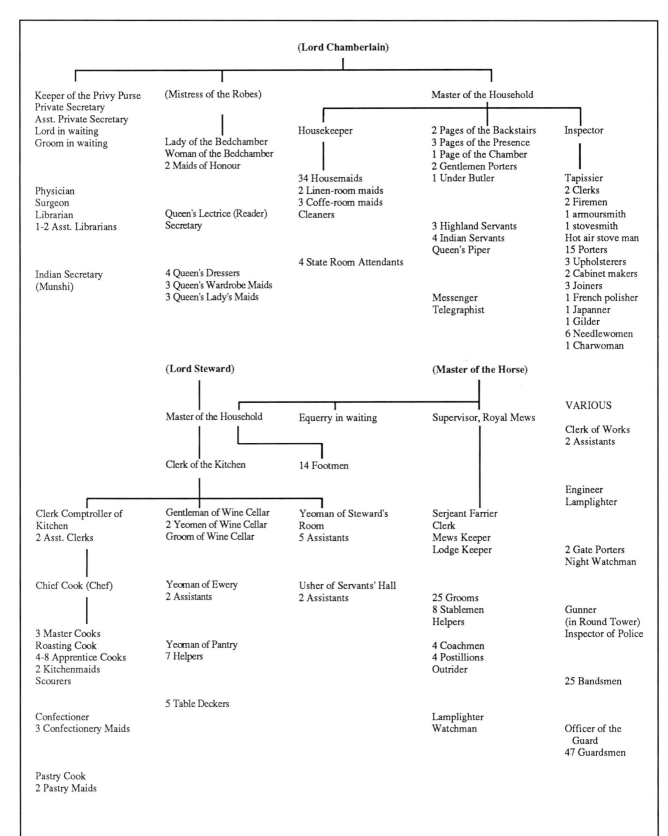

112 The Windsor Household in about 1870-90. Officers in brackets were not normally resident in the Castle. The column under "Various" includes those where the chain of command is uncertain. Gardening and dairy staff are not included.

were moved up to Buckingham Palace and back, horse-drawn all the way in huge, anonymous closed wagons.

On normal days at Windsor food in the Upper Ward was served in seven different places, to the Queen's table, the Household Dining-room, the Equerries' Dining-room, the Steward's Room, the Servants' Hall, the Cooks' room and the kitchenmaids' room. To this, at various times, could be added the nursery, one or more schoolrooms, the coffee room (apparently where royal guests breakfasted or lunched), and the room where the royal band played at dinner; since the room assigned to them had been replaced by the Queen's Private Chapel they played on the terrace outside the dining room window, and mopped up any remaining dessert or drink as they returned into the castle.

Food for all these places was supplied from the Great Kitchen and its dependencies, the Pastry Kitchen, the Green-room, where vegetables were pre-pared, and the Confectionery Kitchen. The organisation needed must have been impressive. The Kitchen as photographed in 1878 (Pl. 110) was still basically the same room as shown by Pyne in 1819, but its walls had been lined with white tiles, its roof whitewashed, and it was presided over by a clock inscribed G IV Rex 1828 and an antlered stag's head. Several hundred brilliantly bur-nished copper containers of all sizes hung round the walls and would "blaze like a million suns through a sulphurous laden fog", according to the anony-mous *Private Life of the Queen* (1897). An unrecorded number of "scourers" kept them in this condition. The floor was sanded, and the sand renewed up to six times a day.

Four of the previously open fireplaces had been filled with closed ranges, but the fireplaces at either end of the room were still used for open-flame roasting, and were big enough to take six rows of joints at a time. At one of them a baron of beef was roasted whenever the royal family was in residence at Christmas. Filling the centre of the room was an enormous steel table, pol-ished till it glittered and rimmed with brass. It was hollow, had hollow steel legs, was filled with steam and used as a hot table. This monumental object was certainly in position by 1848, and it and the ranges were probably installed under Wyatville. The table has gone, but most of the ranges and other early-nineteenth century fittings are still in position (Pl. 111), and have survived the 1992 fire.

At meal times the Kitchen was an inferno of controlled activity. There was a kitchen staff of from thirty to thirty-five people, and although twelve or so of these worked in the subsidiary rooms, there were around twenty in the main Kitchen. The Beefeaters were no longer in evidence; but Pantrymen filed in at one door, bringing in the gold and silver plate, footmen at another to collect the dishes, to quote *Private Life* again, "With the monotonous jangle of the endless chains that turn the spits, mingles the noisy stoking of the many different fires and the clang of the oven doors as they are opened and shut." The cooks ate their own meals in one room, their assistants in another, the kitchenmaids, scourers and apprentices in a third.

112 (left) Household organisation at Windsor in about 1870-90.

It is hard to find out how many people were fed in all, and what the total staff was at the Castle when the Queen was in residence (for much of the Household travelled around with her). There was no single wage or salary book, and many of the relevant accounts or other documents have not found their way to the Royal Archives. Gabriel Tschumi, who came from Switzerland to work as an apprentice cook in the 1890s, says that there was then an indoor staff of over 300. The table on the previous page (Pl. 112), derived from a variety of sources with no claim to complete accuracy, suggests a figure of about two hundred and fifty, but it may not include all the daily staff. In addition there were at least fifty people employed in the Royal Mews and, of course, gardening and outdoor staffs as well; there was a permanent guard based in the Guard-room in the Lower Ward, and a resident gunner in the Round Tower.

A.G. Seymour writes that "Queen Victoria's household servants always seemed to me a happy-go-lucky set. They were not paid high wages, but they made up for it in 'perks'." By the 1890s the government was expressing alarm at the enormous cost of the Royal Household. Even the ageing Queen worried and did her best to be helpful, suggesting, for instance, that she might have fewer varieties of bread at breakfast, or that it was not really necessary for her bed to go off to be mended. But little, if anything, was done until she died.

King Edward VII set to work as soon as he succeeded. The Queen's Indian and Scottish servants were got rid of immediately: all portraits and mementoes of John Brown disappeared almost overnight. The powers of the Master of the Household were increased yet again, the Lord Steward reduced to a purely honorary officer, and his department largely taken over by the Lord Chamberlain. Even so, expenses crept up again; by 1921 the Household was overspending by sixty thousand pounds a year, and a Treasury official was brought in to sort things out. By 1932, according to Gabriel Tschumi, indoor staff were down to about two hundred; by 1954 to one hundred and eighty. There have been successive administrative and financial changes under recent Lord Chamberlains, but anyone moving from the medieval to the modern Royal Household will still find many names that are familiar.

A new feature introduced by the wish of George VI towards the end of the war were the dances given by the staff social clubs, and held in alternate years at Buckingham Palace, and in the Waterloo Chamber and adjacent rooms at Windsor. Members of the royal family were invited, came in an hour or so after the dance had started and took to the floor, each partnered by one of the servants. Similar dances had been held in country houses since at least the early nineteenth century; but as F.J. Corbett, retired Buckingham Palace official, put it in 1956, this was "something that King George V and Queen Mary would never have dreamed of doing". The dances still take place, but today they are given by the Queen.

113 (right) A bird's-eye view of the Lower Ward.

114 (above) Mid-fourteenth century vaulting in the undercroft of the Curfew Tower. From W. St J. Hope *Windsor Castle*.

Threading through the tourists who pour in their thousands through the Lower and Middle Wards is a race apart, distinguishable by their relaxed or purposeful air. They all seem to know each other; they wave or shout greetings as they pass, or stop for a few minutes conversation. They are the people who live or work in the Castle. They are there for all kinds of different reasons: members of the Household, acting or retired, who have houses or apartments there; the archivists of the Royal Archives, shut away in their friendly world of research and coffee-breaks up at least ninety steps in the Round Tower; their fellow-scholars in the Royal Library; the Governor, whose garden, with its miniature waterfall much photographed by tourists, snakes round the ditch and slopes of the Round Tower; the Dean, genial lord of the Lower Ward, and his fellow-Canons; the vergers, choristers and whole administrative world of St George's Chapel; the Military Knights, emerging from their houses on Sundays or special occasions in their handsome uniforms, but otherwise looking, with their neat moustaches and well-kept clothes, like all other decent retired military men; and a network of porters, maintenance men and policemen, helpful and jolly, in a distinctive Windsor way.

This world has existed, with variations, since medieval times. Most of the houses and other buildings which have grown up to contain them have at least a medieval core. But they have been changed, or adapted, added to, partially, or in a few cases completely, rebuilt. Half-timbering has vanished beneath rendering or been encased in brickwork. Sash-windows have replaced casements and leaded lights, bay windows been built out, extra floors added, courtyards filled in; in the nineteenth century Edward Blore, Anthony Salvin and Gilbert Scott were brought in to make bits of the resulting patchwork look medieval again. What they did in the Lower Ward was still only piecemeal; around the dazzling unity of St George's Chapel everything else remains a patchwork, in contrast to the unified world of the Upper Ward. But it is a patchwork of great interest and charm. Anything might come to light; remove some panelling or take down a ceiling, and there, as likely as not, are medieval wall paintings in pristine condition, or a complete roof of magnificent medieval timbers.

All this is the end result of the silting up of simpler, more spacious arrangements

115 (top right) Mid-thirteenth century arcading in the south walk of the Dean's Cloister.

116 (bottom right) Looking from the roof of St George's Chapel down into the Dean's Cloister, with the Deanery and Winchester Tower beyond.

117 (right) The entrance court of the Deanery. The porches mark the position of the former Garter Vestry and Chapter-house.

118 (below) The vault of the porch under the Erary.

119 (far right) Medieval and seventeenth-century filing cabinets in the Erary.

in the fifteenth century. If one could move back to the reign of Henry III one would have found the Lower Ward comparatively open and uncluttered. Around it was the massive outer wall with its great towers, recognisably as it still is today: to the west the present Curfew or Clewer Tower, with its magnificent vaulted basement (Pl. 114), the Garter Tower (lived in then by the Almoner) and the Chancellor's Tower; to the south the Gatehouse, and Henry III's Tower. Within the Gatehouse, the courtyard was dotted with detached buildings, in the earlier medieval fashion: to the west a Great Hall and kitchen (both free-standing), to the east a chapel, and across a court from the chapel the compact mass of Henry III's Royal Lodgings.

The directions issued for lodgings and chapel in 1240 required that "a certain sufficient space be left between the aforesaid lodgings and the chapel itself to make a certain grass plat". The grass plat

112

is still there, forming today the cloister garth of the Dean's Cloister, and claimed to be the oldest lawn in England. But much around it has changed, basically as a result of the founding of the Order of the Garter and its related college a little more than a hundred years later.

The Lodgings were partly destroyed by fire in 1295-6. As the king had by then finally moved up to the Upper Ward they were not repaired. The ruins were removed to give way to the lodgings of the Canons and Priest-vicars of the new College. A cloister walk was formed around the grass plat (Pl. 116). The south wall of this is in fact the north wall of what was Henry III's chapel, and is ornamented with thirteenth-century arcading of a cool simple beauty which can seem like a reproach to the exquisite elaboration of Edward IV's chapel (Pl. 115).

To the east, opening on to the east walk of the Cloister, was built the Chapter-house of the Order of the Garter, with its Vestry adjoining; and the Warden, the precursor of the Dean, was lodged above the Chapter-house. His lodgings were to grow, to absorb the Chapter-house and Vestry, spread to an east wing enclosing a little courtyard (Pl. 117), be extensively re-windowed in

the eighteenth century, and emerge as today's Deanery. To the west a vaulted strong-room was built over a vaulted porch in 1353-4. It was originally known as the Treasury, but soon re-named the Erary (*aerarium* is the Latin for treasury). The porch and its vault are lovely examples of delicate early Perpendicular architecture (Pl. 118); the Erary itself is plainer and more down to earth, as fits its purpose: it was used as a strong-room for the relics and treasures of the College, and later as a store-room for deeds of the College properties: some of these are still kept in a fifteenth-century press, on the drawers of which the names of the different properties are written in a bold seventeenth-century hand (Pl. 119).

120 (right) and 121 (far right) Two views in the Canons' Cloister. Adjoining the Erary a College library was built over the west cloister walk, probably in the fifteenth century. Two-thirds of it was destroyed to make the College Chapter-room, a Victorian Gothic design by Gilbert Scott, but the remaining third is now the Chapter Clerk's office, where oak ceiling bosses carved with fifteenth-century faces and devices look down on the office computers.

114

A fourteenth-century arch in the north wall of the Cloister opens on to a passage leading into the Canons' Cloister. This was originally arranged as in an Oxford or Cambridge college, with doors all round the court and sets of rooms for the Priest-vicars on the ground floor, and the Canons above them. It was, in fact, a miniature precursor of the fifteenth-century quad of Magdalen College, Oxford, with a covered cloister running round the court, as at Magdalen, but built in timber not stone. There were thirteen doors giving access to twenty-six sets of chambers. The simple timber uprights of the covered walk were originally decorated with gothic cusping. A covered way runs across the middle of the court, carrying on the line of the passage from the Dean's Cloister and linking up with the "hundred steps" which zig-zag down the steep northern slopes of the Castle hill to the town.

As the College endowments increased and the Canons grew richer and ultimately, after the Reformation, married and had children, their lodgings grew too small for them. The Priest-vicars were moved out to a new building

in the fifteenth century; rooms were run together, extra rooms built on, and the twenty-six lodgings ended up as eight Canons' houses, grouped round their charmingly domestic court and full of variety owing to the different ways in which they had been altered (Pls. 120, 121). One of these houses absorbed the College Library for a time; one pushed out the bay window which is still a picturesque feature of the Dean's Cloister (Pl. 123); all of them retain bits and pieces of medieval detailing, and in some fragments of medieval wall-paintings have come to light. The most remarkable of them was only uncovered a few years ago, in the upper story of a house which is now the office of the conference centre known as St George's House (Pl. 122).

As adapted, the Canons' Cloister could only house eight of the twelve Canons and extra houses had to be built for them, to the west of the Cloister.

Some of these have been abolished, but a picturesque and varied group still runs west from the Canons' Cloister along the Castle wall. A big hipped-roof house, probably built in 1684 by Canon Turner, joins on to a red-brick façade built in 1661 by Canon Hall (Pl. 124), another house incorporating precious fragments of the medieval Great Hall, and ends with a boldly-designed half-timbered building of about 1500, partly demolished and heavily restored in 1874 (Pl. 126). This last was not built as a canon's house; at one time it was divided into two houses for the schoolmasters who taught grammar and music to the choir-boys.

The Priest-vicars, having been ejected from their original lodgings, were moved into another building,

which has long since been demolished, and finally re-housed in some style in what became known, from its shape, as the Horseshoe Cloister, to the west of the Chapel. It was built in 1479-81, on an unusual polygonal plan; originally it joined on to the west front of St George's. It contained twenty-one houses, of brick-filled half-timber, linked by a timber cloister.

Under Henry VIII the thirteen Priest-vicars began to be replaced by a new group known as minor canons, slightly higher in status and rather better paid. The two groups existed side by side for a time, but in the end the Priest-vicars disappeared. The minor canons may initially have lived in the Horseshoe Cloister, but their number fell from thirteen to seven, and this, combined per-haps with absenteeism among them and the Canons, meant that they began to move back into the Canons' Cloister and its adjuncts. This movement was fi-nalised when the members of both were gradually reduced to four, following an Act of Parliament in 1840. By the end of the eighteenth century the Horseshoe Cloister was known as the Singing Men's Cloister, and most of it was presumably occupied by the singing-clerks, as some may have been from the beginning and much of it still is today. By then the whole complex had be-come dilapidated, if rather charming, as one of Sandby's watercolours shows (Pl. 127). In 1870 it was "restored" by Gilbert Scott. The restoration incorporated a certain number of old timbers and accurately re-created the

119

original detail of the cloister but was virtually a complete re-building. The fine fifteenth-century hall to the north, perhaps originally used by the priest vicars, was adapted as the new Chapter Library. One may regret the haphazard picturesqueness of the buildings as depicted by Sandby, but the end result (Pl. 128) was, after all, a handsome composition given new importance by a big gable and two octagonal towers.

The curved roofs which top the two towers in the Horseshoe Cloister seem to be inspired by the roof of the seventeenth-century belfry turret which used to surmount the Curfew Tower, and was further embellished by a pedimented clock face, added in 1756. All this was extinguished when Anthony Salvin put a new roof like a candle snuffer on top of it in 1862-3. It was clearly influenced by Viollet-le-Duc's restoration, planned in 1855, of the Tour de Trésor at Carcassonne. Viollet-le-Duc's restoration of the walled town of Carcassonne had caught the imagination of contemporary architects, especially its most debatable feature, the high roofs which he put on the towers, on dubious evidence, but much to mid-nineteenth century taste. (There is no evidence that Salvin's roof derived from Napoleon III's visit to Windsor in 1855, as is sometimes stated.) Once again, one can regret the charm of the extinguished belfry, but appreciate the lift which Salvin's roof gives to the skyline of the Castle (Pl. 129).

129 (top left) The Curfew Tower seen from the town.
130 (bottom left) Inside the Curfew Tower, showing the medieval framework inserted to support the Chapel bells. From Pyne *Royal Residences*.
131 (above) After Sunday service. Three Military Knights outside their houses today.

The belfry was based on a medieval framework (Pl. 130), which is still there under the roof, along with the new clock made by John Davis of Windsor, installed in 1689, and the supporting scaffolding of mighty beams built to support it. The timber frame was inserted into the tower in 1477-82, when the bells were moved there from a tower by the gatehouse to the Lower Ward.

The Dean and Chapter's territory ceases to the south of St George's Chapel, and the rest of the Lower Ward is occupied by the Gatehouse, guard-rooms and the houses of the Military Knights. The latter had been founded as the twenty-six Poor Knights by Edward III but had never been properly endowed, and had all but disappeared until Henry VIII decided to re-found them (with the number reduced to thirteen). In the 1550s Queen Mary built the row of houses with little front gardens where they still live (Pl. 131). The eastern half of these was in fact a re-modelling of fourteenth-century lodgings built for the singing-clerks; the western six were new, and their Governor lived (and still lives) in the tower in the middle, the former belfry tower of St George's.

By the late eighteenth century there was nothing very knightly about the Poor Knights, as they were still called, for they had been infiltrated by retired Windsor shopkeepers or Eton schoolmasters. These were gradually replaced by

132 (left) A group of Military Knights in 1891.

133 (above) The Winchester Tower, where Jeffrey Wyatville lived during the re-modelling of the Castle. From J. Ashton *Illustrations of Windsor Castle* (1841).

veteran officers of the Napoleonic Wars, who disliked both being called Poor Knights and wearing their traditional red cloak. William IV accordingly changed their name to the Military Knights, and gave them the red and blue uniform and gold-braided cocked hats which they still wear on dress occasions (Pl. 132). In 1795 George III had inaugurated a fellow body of Naval Knights, but it was not a success. The new knights were quarrelsome and hard-drinking, and were disbanded in 1892, owing to "irredeemable discord" between the two services.

In the almost total absence of the royal family during most of the eighteenth century, and its long absences subsequently (for even Queen Victoria was only there for at most six months a year), the resident aristocracy at the Castle was made up of the Dean and Canons in the Lower Ward, the families living in the towers grouped around the Middle Ward (Pl. 133), and, in the eighteenth century, by the old ladies who were given grace-and-favour apartments in the Upper Ward, before royalty returned to it — the "few antique dowagers, who had each their domiciles in some lone turret of that spacious square", as Charles Knight puts it.

The Round Tower was lived in by the Governor-cum-Constable of the Castle, as it had been from at least the seventeenth century. It made a spacious enough house, once one had climbed up to it (Pl. 134), with its rooms grouped around a small court and a sensational view from the windows pierced through its mighty outer wall. Prince Rupert, who was Governor under Charles II, conducted scientific experiments up there, and arranged arms and armour in decorative patterns on the walls of its fourteenth century hall; a new arrangement was installed under the Duke of St Albans in the early eighteenth century,

134 (left) The stairs to the Round Tower, as re-built in 1439-40.

135 (above) The Norman Gate and its extension in the Round Tower ditch, before Wyatville's re-modelling. From the water colour by Paul Sandby.

much admired by Georgian tourists. The Governship later became a sinecure, usually held by a member of the royal family, and the Round Tower was used to provide supplementary accommodation for royal guests, until the Royal Archive was moved into it in 1911. In the last few years the empty space behind Wyatville's upper wall has been filled by two extra floors for the archives, supported on mighty steel columns rising up through the courtyard.

For at least a hundred years the Norman Gate or Tower between the Middle and Upper Wards, and a wing adjoining it, opening on to the ditch around the Round Tower, were occupied by the Lady Housekeeper. Lady Mary Coke thought it "one of the prettiest apartments I ever saw" in 1764, by when the wing on the ditch had been re-fronted and given sash windows and a pediment (Pl. 135). It was all restored, re-modelled and made gothic again by Wyatville. Under Victoria and later it was occupied by members of the Household, including Queen Victoria's Private Secretaries, General Grey and Sir Henry Ponsonby, and Sir Dighton Probyn, Keeper of the Privy Purse to Edward VII. It was Probyn who made the rock garden on the Round Tower mount, bringing lumps of Norfolk Car stone from Sandringham for the purpose.

One can get an underside view of this life in the Castle from the memories of those who lived or visited there as children. They explored the basement passages which criss-crossed below the Castle, skated on the Frogmore lake and made expeditions to the grotto in the Home Park which they believed to be an exact model of the famous Black Hole of Calcutta. When the Queen was in residence they played with the royal children in the Corridor, or were invited to have tea, and delicious sweets from the Confectionery, in their nurseries or schoolroom. They had lessons in the Royal Riding-School under a fat German riding-master, wandered among the carriages in the carriage-yard, and looked with envy at the "tiny barouche with every detail perfect down to silver gilt crowns, but only just large enough to hold a small child", as Louisa Grey records. Eton boys came up the hill to have tea with them; at services in St George's Chapel they gazed at the Military Knights "with their cocked hats, everyone of them looking like a Field Marshal"; at nights they listened to the Last Post, sounded on the bugles of the Castle garrison. On the Fifth of November, an effigy of Guy Fawkes was hung from the Curfew Tower. The Greys of the Norman Tower made friends with the Phippses in the Henry III Tower (their father was Keeper of the Privy Purse), and the children of the two families slid on their bottoms down the slopes of the Round Tower mound, while the tourists watched them from over the wall.

Today the Norman Gate is lived in by the Governor of the Castle, the Winchester Tower by the Queen's Private Secretary, and the Henry III Tower is divided into five grace-and-favour apartments.

136 (right) Looking up the Long Walk to the Castle. The Walk was laid out by Charles II in 1680.

6 Royal Recreations

P rince Pückler-Muskau, the German princeling who travelled indefatigably around England and Ireland in the 1820s, was especially taken by Windsor Great Park, because of its enormous size. It realised his ideal, as a private kingdom "within the bounds of which you can live and do what you like, without privation and constraint; hunt, fish, ride, drive, without ever feeling cramped; in which you never, except just at the entrance-gates, come to a point at which you remark, Here is a boundary".

The Great Park's existence as a private world for the royal family to enjoy themselves in dates back to the time it was first enclosed in the eleventh century. By about 1365 it had acquired more or less its present size and shape. But its landscape was very different from the mixture of fields, plantations, lakes and Georgian-style parkland which makes up most of it today. It was all heath or scrub, dotted with self-sown oaks and beeches, over and among which the deer roamed. One can get some idea of its character from the drawings made by Paul Sandby in its wilder parts in the 1760s and 1770s.

Although the main purpose of the park was for the king to hunt in, it was sometimes used for other purposes. In 1278 Edward I gave a tournament there, a medieval anticipation of the polo tournaments to be held on Smith's Lawn in this century. There were thirty-eight combatants, ten of whom were described as "more worthy" than the rest. These worthier knights had gilded helms, the rest wore helms of silver.

The Little Park (later known as the Home Park), immediately adjacent to the Castle, was in existence in a small way as early as the thirteenth century, and by the time it was surveyed in 1607 contained 280 acres and 240 fallow deer (Pl. 137). It was originally separated from the Great Park by a strip of land which did not belong to the Crown; the two properties were only joined together in comparatively recent years.

The King's father, Henry III, had built a manor house or lodge towards the southern end of the Great Park in the 1240s. It was a sizeable moated building, and had stew-ponds attached to it, stocked with pike, bream and other fish. Edward I preferred it to the Castle, and it was much used by Edward II and Richard II. The moated buildings are still shown in a survey made in 1607, but were probably in decay by then. The site is now the little Moat Island on the northern side of Virginia Water. It was the first of a series of houses or lodges which were built and re-built in both parks over the centuries, as retreats for the monarch or residences for other members of the royal family, or for the Ranger of the Park and his assistants. Adjacent to one of these buildings, Cranbourn Lodge, Queen Elizabeth had thirteen acres of the Great Park planted with oaks in 1580, on Lord Burghley's advice, to provide future timber for ships. Some of the oaks survive, and are perhaps the earliest datable plantation in England. Charles II followed on with the great elm avenue of the Broad

137 (right) Castle Home and Great Park in the early eighteenth century

128

Walk, planted in 1680 to lead from the Castle to the Great Park. It became the most prominent feature in the Park, and indeed still is, though Charles II's trees had to be felled and re-planted with planes and chestnuts in the 1940s. Charles II loved both parks, and spent long hours walking and racing in and around them (Pl. 138), as did his niece Queen Anne, who when she got too fat and old to ride would take a horse and chaise at great speed across country, driving "furiously, like Jehu" according to Jonathan Swift's description.

The Great Park was looked after by a Ranger. He or she usually had a

house there, and when the monarch was not in residence at the Castle used the Park very much as their own private property. Under Queen Anne the Ranger was the formidable and quarrelsome Duchess of Marlborough; she lived in what came to be called Cumberland Lodge, a mid-seventeenth century house built during the Civil War, when the Great Park was temporarily sold off in lots. The Duchess enlarged the Lodge, and while she was Ranger further avenues were planted, including the long drive known as the Queen's Avenue, or Queen Anne's Ride, which still runs for three miles or so through the western section of the park.

Cumberland Lodge owes its name to George III's uncle, the Duke of Cumberland. He was Ranger from 1746 to 1765. With him and his nephew, also created Duke of Cumberland, who succeeded him as Ranger, the Great Park entered a new phase. When it was primarily a hunting park the first interest of the Ranger and his keepers had been to preserve the deer and the trees that gave them shelter; consideration of beauty was of no great importance, nor did privacy rank especially high, as long as the deer were not interfered with. The two Dukes of Cumberland, influenced by contemporary movements in landscape gardening, set about creating a secret paradise of glades, woodland and lakes, dotted with romantic buildings, all deliberately built, planned and planted for visual effect. Such a paradise had to be private to be effective, and the elder Duke earned himself much unpopularity by shutting local people out of it.

Much of the planting of the park today dates from this time, but its most obvious legacy is the great lake at Virginia Water (Pl. 140). This was originally formed in about 1750 with the help of the architect Henry Flitcroft and the Duke's protégé Thomas Sandby, and later enlarged by Sandby and the next Duke. The elder Duke had a Chinese barge, the *Mandarin*, made to sail up and down on this, "as rich and gay as carving, gilding and Japanning can make it", as

138 (above) Charles II watching a horse race on Datchet Mead, below the Castle. From an anonymous contemporary painting at Windsor.

139 (right) The Duke of Cumberland's yacht *Mandarin* on Virginia Water, with the Belvedere beyond.

140 (following page) A view on Virginia Water.

one description put it (Pl. 139), and built a little Chinese pavilion on the island site where Henry III's manor had been, joined to the mainland by a Chinese bridge. On top of the slope to the south of the lake Flitcroft designed a triangular tower, with octagonal turrets at its corners, known as the Belvedere. When the original sand-and-clay dam of Virginia Water collapsed in 1768, a new one was built by Thomas Sandby, by now Deputy Ranger, with the help of a surveyor in the Office of Woods and Forests, Charles Cole. Sandby embellished the dam with rocks and grottoes. At about the same time he replaced a wooden bridge across the lake, designed by Flitcroft, with the pleasing stone bridge which is still there (Pl. 141).

By the time the younger Duke died in 1790, George III was living more and more at Windsor. The two brothers did not get on well, and the Duke made difficulties about the King hunting in the park. So when he died the King appointed himself Ranger, and all subsequent monarchs have done the same — or, in the case of queens, appointed their husbands.

George III enjoyed riding and hunting in both parks, but he also embarked on a more practical recreation: he took up farming, and became known as "Farmer George". There had already been sporadic farming in odd fields dotted over the Great Park, but in 1791 George III employed Nathaniel Kent, a land agent and author of a work on estate management, to create two consolidated farms, Norfolk Farm and Gloucestershire, or Flemish, Farm, and design and construct model farm-buildings on them. The result of the work of the Dukes of Cumberland and Sandby on the one hand and George III and Nathaniel Kent on the other was that the Great Park assumed the character of mixed woodland, parkland and farmland that it has today.

A View of the Mandarine Yatcht and Belvedere belonging to His

What was added by George IV has largely disappeared, and was more a matter of individual buildings than changes to the landscape. But if the legendary figure of Herne the Hunter, antlers sprouting from his head, haunts the surviving wild places of Windsor Forest, the ghost of George IV, obese and voluptuous like the Emperor Nero in his barge, should haunt Virginia Water, where the denizens of outer suburbia now exercise their dogs. He adored the Great Park; it was his jealously-guarded Elysium, where he felt safe from his enemies. Around and on the lake he lived an outdoor life as extraordinary and, in its way, as stifling as in the lush interiors, heated to boiling point, of the so-called "cottage" in the Park where he lived.

141 (previous page) The bridge across the west end of Virginia Water, designed by Thomas Sandby in about 1770.

142 (above) Royal Lodge. From the engraving in Huish *Memoirs of George IV* (1831).

This was originally called Lower Lodge, and was a very modest house, with a hipped roof, dormers, shutters and a pedimented doorcase. Thomas Sandby had lived there as Deputy Ranger. The Prince originally intended to use it as a temporary residence while the neighbouring Cumberland Lodge was being enlarged for him. Work on adapting it started in November 1812, with John Nash as the architect, and as usually happened with the Prince Regent, once he started building he could not stop. After a year or so the idea of his living in Cumberland Lodge was dropped; and when he finally moved into his cottage, at the end of 1816, over fifty thousand pounds had been spent on it. At least thirty thousand pounds followed, after the Prince succeeded as George IV in 1820, and lived at Royal Lodge, as it was now called, while Windsor Castle was being re-modelled.

Sandby's little house had by now totally disappeared. Initially it was re-modelled as a picturesque cottage *orné* with a thatched roof and a thatched verandah supported on rustic timber posts; but the thatched roof hatched more thatched roofs, the cottage grew, the verandah spread, a conservatory was added (Pl. 142); then Wyatville took over from Nash, replaced the thatched roofs with slate and made more additions.

"It was a dwelling place at once royal and rustic, on the outside the simplicity of a cottage, within the rarest union of comfort, elegance and magnificence," wrote Princess Lieven, the wife of the Russian ambassador. She knew what she was talking about, for the Lievens, the Austro-Hungarian Esterhazys, the King's honorary mistress (it is questionable whether he ever slept with her) Lady Conyngham and her complaisant husband formed the core of the "Cottage Côterie" who stayed constantly at Royal Lodge. Other descriptions comment on the luxury of its rooms. There is nothing to back up their descriptions, for no plans, architect's drawings or illustrations of the interior survive.

George IV also did a good deal elsewhere in the Park. Wyatville re-built all the entrance lodges for him; and behind one of them, Sandpit-Gate Lodge, he formed a menagerie, which gradually increased until it contained, among much else, monkeys, kangaroos, a zebra, a leopard, a llama, ostriches, eagles and a giraffe. On Virginia Water he re-built the Chinese pavilion on a larger scale, to the designs of Frederick Crace (Pl. 143), put up a series of ornamental tents next to it, enlarged the Belvedere, re-named it Fort Belvedere and built a bastion in front of it, equipped with the Duke of Cumberland's cannon from Cumberland Lodge. He re-modelled or totally re-built Sandby's rockwork on the dam, so that it looked like a small Alpine waterfall, surprisingly transported into the Surrey landscape (Pl. 144).

His most curious addition was a little further along the lake from the waterfall. The Sultan of Sokoto sent him three parrots and four ostriches for his menagerie; the Pasha of Egypt sent him a giraffe (Pl. 149); the Bashaw of Tripoli sent him thirty-five and a half marble columns, twenty-five marble pedestals, ten massive pieces of cornice, five "faces", two statues without heads or feet and various other bits and pieces, all removed from the ruins of the Roman city of Leptis Magna, lost in the desert seventy miles from Tripoli.

The gift seems to have been suggested to the Bashaw by Colonel Hanmer Warrington, the English consul at Tripoli. The Bashaw was amenable; he was happy to please the English, and although the Roman columns were periodically cut up by the local Arabs to make grindstones they must otherwise have seemed useless to him. Warrington was encouraged by Commander W.H. Smyth, who commanded a ship in the English fleet then in the Mediterranean. The Colonial Secretary authorised Warrington to proceed, and in November 1817 Smyth loaded whatever he could fit into his ship, listed it and sailed off to England by way of Malta.

When the ship arrived the Prince Regent showed little interest in the cargo. The marbles were unloaded and the Admiralty ordered them to be

handed over to the Trustees of the British Museum. They lay neglected in its courtyard for the next six years. Finally, in August 1824, Sir Charles Long wrote to the Museum communicating: "His Majesty's commands that the Columns and Fragments deposited in the Courtyard of the Museum should be placed at the disposal of his architect, Mr Jeffry Wyatt, to whom His Majesty has given further directions concerning them." In fact it was not until after a further two years that a detachment of Royal Engineers moved the columns from London to Virginia Water.

Sir Charles Long was a trustee of the Museum; as so often with George IV one can probably see his inspiration and suggestion behind the ruined "Temple of Augustus" which now rose on the edge of Virginia Water, under Wyatville's directions (Pl. 145). A double row of broken columns, some with capitals and fragments of entablature on them, forms a kind of nave, open to the sky, which leads to where an arch has been tunnelled under the public road; through this is a further semi-circle of columns, cut into the slopes below Fort Belvedere. The capitals have a scraped look (apart from the Corinthian capitals in the semi-circle, which seem not to have come from Leptis) because the foliage which decorated their bases had been cut off by vandals before they left Tripoli. A few Roman statues, already in the King's possession, were disposed among the ruins; English vandals got to work on them, they were finally removed, and have long since disappeared.

Everything was oriented on the lake. The King could disport himself on

143 (above) George IV's Chinese Pavilion on Virginia Water. From a drawing by S.S. Teulon, 1860, probably made in connection with repairs to the Pavilion.

144 (right) The cascade at the east end of Virginia Water.

this with his party, disembark at a landing stage (Pl. 146), where a flight of steps led up through four pedestals decorated with Medusa heads (four of the "faces" from Leptis); walk across a grassy meadow to the ruins, and either picnic in them or walk or be carried up through them to Fort Belvedere. On 12 August, 1829, his last birthday before his death, the cannon fired a salute from its bastion, and he gave a luncheon party there.

The lake featured prominently in the pattern of life at Royal Lodge. The King liked to go there every day during the summer, fish from one boat while a band played to him and his party in the other, and lunch in the Chinese Temple or the adjoining tents. He drove, too, all round the park, especially to Sandpit-Gate Lodge to visit his menagerie, and drink a glass of cherry-gin with his favourite cockatoo on his shoulder. At dinner in the Lodge a band played in

145 (above) The Roman Ruins on Virginia Water, constructed in 1826 of fragments brought from Leptis Magna, near Tripoli.

146 (right) Gorgons' heads from Leptis Magna on the landing stage by the Ruins.

the adjoining conservatory (when he asked his seven-year-old niece Princess Victoria what she would like them to play, the tactful child answered "God Save the King"); sometimes there were diversions like a visit from a troupe of Tyrolese dancers or a deputation of Red Indians. "We led a lazy and agreeable life there, always in the King's society," wrote Princess Lieven. "Many promenades in the forest, on the lake, sometimes dinners under tents, always music in the evenings, and in everything a habit of unspoiled magnificence which left behind the sentiment of *une charmante béatitude*."

But she added: "I will not say that this state of bliss was not sometimes exchanged for great boredom." The Duke of Wellington described how he "felt for three days exactly as if I was at the end of the world; and literally speaking, I saw nobody excepting our own company and two men who, attracted by the music on the water, came down to the bank to see and were driven off by the

150 (right) "The Copper Horse". Statue by Richard Westmacot, showing George III on horseback, erected at the end of the Long Walk in 1831.

151 (far right, above) The Royal Stable and Riding School, on the edge of the Home Park. From the watercolour by C.R. Stanley.

152 (far right, below) Distribution of Royal Bounty in the Riding School, 1846. From the watercolour by Joseph Nash.

keepers, in the same manner as the people of Constantinople are driven from the sight of the Grand Signor". The park was both a paradise and a prison; George IV stayed in it because, swollen as he was with gout and dropsy, immensely fat, his face covered in greasepaint to conceal his wrinkles, and subject to constant merciless attacks and cartoons in the press, both political and personal, he could not bear to be looked at. Keepers were posted everywhere to ensure his privacy; double ring fences surrounded the Lodge and other sensitive places. Of the four and a half years from June 1824, he spent three and a half at the Lodge. His ministers were driven mad by having to come down there and endure rambling, two-hour monologues or interminable

142

drives and excursions before they could get a decision out of him. The more he hid himself, the more he was criticised; the more he was criticised, the more he hid himself. But the cartoonists still pursued him; when his giraffe, whom he loved dearly, died they made fun of him and it (Pl. 148); when he employed a pretty actress, Clare Austen, to read to him, Gillray drew her as a park deer, looking at him with big eyes.

The King's most prominent contribution to the Great Park had nothing to do with life at the Lodge. At the end of the Long Walk he caused a statue of his father on horseback to be erected (Pl. 150). The sculptor was Richard Westmacott, and it became known, because of the material of which it was made, as the Copper Horse. It was designed to be seen from the Castle three miles away, and therefore had to be, as Wyatville put it, "colossal". Wyatville designed a plinth of piled-up rocks for it, twenty-seven feet high, above which horse and rider rose about the same height again. (The inspiration was probably the rock-based statue of Peter the Great which Alexander I had installed in

St Petersburg in 1782). It is an odd experience, when walking through the park from the direction of Virginia Water, to see the huge beast and its rider unexpectedly rising above the trees.

George IV laid the foundation stone of the plinth on his last birthday. The statue was not installed until after his death, in October 1831. A lunch was given to twelve people inside the horse, and it was then closed up; according to A.G. Seymour, whose father was amongst the lunchers, a ladder was left inside it by mistake, and is presumably still there.

By then Royal Lodge had all but disappeared. William IV pulled it down soon after the death of his brother, all but the big dining-room designed by Wyatville, which had been started a few months before George IV's death. Some of the details were re-used in Adelaide Cottage, a little cottage *orné* in the Home Park, which Queen Adelaide used as a terminus for walks from the Castle. The Chinese pavilion survived into Queen Victoria's reign, but today there is no trace of it, the tents or the menagerie.

Royal building activities had, in fact, shifted from the Great to the Home Park. The Duchess of Kent had moved into Frogmore House, inside the park

153 (above) Queen Victoria planting an oak tree in memory of Prince Albert in the Great Park, 25 November, 1863.

154 (right) Keepers, Beaters and "Jägers" of Prince Albert, 1852. From the photograph by Brunell.

144

below the Castle, and on the edge of it William planned the great complex of stables, carriage-houses and riding-school which was finally built by Queen Victoria shortly after his death (Pls. 151-2). Wyatville designed them, but died soon after they had been started, and they were finished off by Henry Ashton, who had been his assistant.

Queen Victoria rode a good deal in the Great Park, and made Prince Albert its Ranger. He filled the position energetically and effectively, re-built the farms and enjoyed shooting in the park (Pl. 154), and coursing in it with his greyhound Eos. But much of his energy, as far as the Parks were concerned, was spent on embellishing the Home Park and making it private. At the beginning of the Queen's reign it was still crossed by several public foot-paths and used for recreation by the Windsor people. By giving its northern section, next to the river, to the town, the Prince was able to close the rest without too much ill-feeling. The kind of fantastic architecture which appealed to George IV was not to the taste of either the Prince or his wife; they preferred useful buildings made ornamental. Most of the Home Park was enclosed for farming and two pretty model-farms and an even prettier aviary were built

SECTION OF ROYAL
DAIRY.

LOOKING SOUTH.

SCALE 1/4 in. to 1 Foot.

(Pl. 155). But the most elaborate of the Home Park buildings is the Royal Dairy. This was designed in 1858 by John Thomas (Pl. 156). It has rows of decorated basins, an open timber roof, richly coloured Minton tiles, painted decoration and stained glass. The result is an interior so overwhelmingly Victorian that it seems almost too good to be true

Prince Albert laid out and planted the steep ground to the north of the Castle to form what became known as the "Slopes". The Queen used to take exercise there, and the Household was also allowed to use the area, but the Queen disliked meeting them; if they saw her coming they had to make a quick retreat or hide in the bushes. There was another garden down at Frogmore, skilfully laid out in the late eighteenth century with a winding lake and plantations. The Queen was fond of visiting it, not least because it was at Frogmore that she had built the great mausoleum where Prince Albert, and later she herself, were buried, next to the smaller mausoleum of the Duchess of Kent.

Windsor Great Park came back into prominence when the Prince of Wales moved into Fort Belvedere in 1930 (Pl. 157), and his brother the Duke of York into a re-enlarged Royal Lodge in 1932. The Duke of York became an ambitious and knowledgeable landscape gardener, and as King George VI encouraged the Deputy Ranger to create what became the Savill Gardens, to the north-east of Virginia Water. This was started in 1932, and today is perhaps the major public attraction in the Great Park.

But undoubtedly it is horses with which the general public especially associate the royal family as far as outdoor life at Windsor is concerned. Royalty has, of course, ridden and hunted in the two parks since medieval times, and Queen Victoria in her early and middle years was an indefatigable and dashing

155 (top left) The Aviary and Poultry Farm. From the 1845 watercolour by C.R. Stanley.
156 (bottom left) Design byJohn Thomas for the Royal Dairy, 1858.
157 (above) The Prince of Wales (later Edward VIII), before Fort Belvedere.

horsewoman. But horse-based activities at Windsor naturally declined in her old age; subsequent monarchs were more interested in racing than riding, and it is only with the present Queen, her husband and children, that horses have come back into their own at Windsor. The Royal Windsor Horse Show was inaugurated in 1944, with Princesses Elizabeth and Margaret Rose, as they then were, competing. Carriage driving became a feature of the Show, and the International Carriage Driving Championships have been attached to it since 1971 (Pl. 159). In 1956 the Duke of Edinburgh was among the founders of the Household Brigade Polo Club at Smith's Lawn in the Great Park, where the Prince of Wales played until the summer of 1992 (Pl. 158).

158 (top) The Prince of Wales on Smith's Lawn, Windsor Great Park.
159 (above) The Duke of Edinburgh driving at Windsor Horse Show.
160 (right) St George's Hall after the fire in November 1992.

7 The Fire and the Future

In November 1992 Windsor Castle caught fire. The probable cause was an electric light-bulb left burning too close to the curtains in the Private Chapel. The flames moved rapidly up to the ceiling and through it into the roofs. They spread at frightening speed, and by the time the fire-engines had arrived had taken an inextinguishable hold. All that could be done was to isolate the portions on fire, and let them burn themselves out.

The fire burnt for over twenty-four hours. The flaming Castle on its hill was a sensational sight, especially at night. Fortunately, since the rooms in the Upper Ward were in process of being re-wired, a considerable proportion of the pictures and contents were in store. Volunteer help quickly removed anything of value that was thought to be in danger. The Duke of York was amongst those who joined in the work, and the Lord Chamberlain climbed up a ladder to help remove the Lawrences from their frames in the Waterloo Chamber. Watchers on television saw the gigantic carpet from the same room, originally woven in Agra in 1894, moving into the courtyard along with dozens of helpers, like an enormous caterpillar. Little in the way of contents of value was destroyed; the worst losses were a large picture of George III reviewing his troops, by Sir William Beechey, and a massive Gothic sideboard, probably designed by Augustus Welby Pugin, both in the Dining-room; and the organ in the gallery between St George's Hall and the Private Chapel.

The damage to fabric and decoration was much more serious. Only the north-east corner of the Upper Ward was involved, but it was a big corner and contained some of the finest rooms in the Castle. Apart from the Private Chapel, where the fire started, the rooms damaged included St George's Hall, the Grand Reception Room, the Octagon Room in the Brunswick Tower, the Dining-room, the Crimson Drawing-room, one end of the Green Drawing-room and the Great Kitchen.

None of these rooms was completely annihilated, though some were damaged much more badly than others. Wall decorations, in many cases, were blackened by smoke or damaged by water, rather than destroyed. Ceilings collapsed, but they were of plaster, and plaster does not burn; they smashed into fragments, but the fragments were capable of re-assembly. Even the great chandeliers, which collapsed with the ceilings and lay in tangled wreckage on the floor, were not past restoration, as has been shown by the restoration of chandeliers damaged in the less serious fire at Hampton Court in 1986.

What should be done? Most of the damaged rooms could be restored in such a way that to the layman's eye it would look, in a few years' time, as though no fire had ever taken place. Such a restoration would involve a combination of retaining what was not damaged, re-assembling what could be re-assembled, repairing what could be repaired, replacing the rest, including all damaged fabrics or charred woodwork, and then re-installing the original

161 (top right) The Castle burning.

162 (bottom right) Looking through the window of the burnt-out Crimson Drawing-room.

150

contents. Restoration work of this nature would call for extensive research, high levels of craftsmanship and a sensitive feeling for the quality of the damaged rooms. The result would not be a fake, but a repair, however extensive, in that it would involve filling in gaps in damaged rooms rather than creating completely new rooms to look like old ones. Even so, one cannot pretend that the rooms would end up the same as they were before. Work done in the late twentieth century, however skilfully or sympathetically, cannot be exactly the same as work done in the early nineteenth century: something of the difference in outlook, background and methods between the two periods will always creep in.

That being so, one must ask why the differences should not express themselves as differences, rather than self-effacingly trying to behave as though they did not exist. Or, more positively, why should an event as dramatic and catastrophic as the great fire of 1992 be censored out of the Castle's history? Wren's St Paul's arose in place of the charred ruins of Old St Paul's, after the Great Fire of 1666. In 1834, the Palace of Westminster went up in a blaze even more sensational than that at Windsor Castle, and was replaced by Barry's neo-Gothic masterpiece. The parallel is not complete; St Paul's and the Houses of Parliament were far more extensively damaged than Windsor Castle, and one must allow for more ruthless attitudes in earlier centuries towards the replacement of old buildings. But today do we have to go to the other extreme?

Windsor Castle has grown and changed century by century. One can enjoy, as a result, the noble fragments of Henry III's chapel; Edward III's towers and vaulted undercrofts; Edward IV's fretted St George's Chapel; the lantern glazing of Henry VII's wing and Elizabeth's great chimneypiece; the work of Verrio and Gibbons for Charles II; George III's Burial Chamber and embellishments to St George's Chapel; George IV's sensational re-modellings; the Clewer Tower, Prince Albert Memorial Chapel, Salvin's State Staircase, the Private Audience Chamber, and a good deal else created under Queen Victoria; even the King's Beasts cutting the skyline of the Lower Ward, under George V; and then what? Embellishments and improvements in Windsor Great Park there have indeed been under the present Queen and her father, but new work in the Castle itself has been virtually confined to Sir Hugh Casson's re-decoration of the Duke of Edinburgh's study, some guest suites and the Private Chapel in the Private Apartments — honourable work by a distinguished architect, but of its nature of minor importance and, in the case of the Private Chapel, already destroyed. Unlike Hampton Court Palace, which went into mothballs in the eighteenth century, Windsor Castle is still a living and working royal residence. The fire gives an opportunity to add a late-twentieth century layer to the Castle's complexity, and give Crown and Government the opportunity for some intelligent patronage, and a little creative fun into the bargain.

163 (right) The morning after: the Queen visits the Castle.

It is worth looking at the damaged rooms in separate groups: the Crimson

and Green Drawing-rooms, the Private Dining-room and Chapel, the Great Kitchen, the Grand Reception Room and, finally, St George's Hall. All have different characteristics, and perhaps call for different treatment.

The Crimson and Green Drawing-rooms form part of a sequence of three drawing-rooms conceived and executed as a whole within a few years. They are George IV's most personal legacy to the Castle. They express his own private taste, and were amongst the most important examples of sumptuous late-neoclassical domestic interiors in England. They were designed to set off contents of superb quality which were not destroyed in the fire. The White Drawing-room survives unscathed; only one end of the Green Drawing-room has been damaged; and although the Crimson Drawing-room has suffered badly (Pl. 162), parts of it are still more or less intact. There are strong arguments for restoring the rooms as far as is possible to what they were before the fire — possibly even to what they were at the death of George IV.

The Private Dining-room and Chapel are in a different category. They were out-of-sequence rooms, each unlike anything else in the State or Private Apartments. Although by no means without interest, they lacked the outstanding quality of the drawing-rooms, and their furnishings and contents did not relate to them in the same way — with the exception of the Gothic furniture in the Dining-room, and the most important piece of this, the sideboard, has been destroyed. They and the Octagon Room suffered much the most serious damage from the fire. Any reconstruction would be almost entirely new work. It would be better to replace them with rooms of new design.

Only the roof of the Great Kitchen was damaged. Its plaster cove and most of its medieval timbers were destroyed, but the later timber arches beneath the cove survive. It is an extraordinary room, and ought to be restored to its appearance before the fire.

The Grand Reception Room, as perhaps the most brilliantly creative example of the opulent Louis XV revival of the 1820s and 1830s, was arguably the most interesting and impressive of George IV's rooms at Windsor. Its walls, with their boiseries and abundance of decorative plasterwork, survive smoke-blackened but more or less intact. Most of the equally lavish ceiling is down, but much could be reconstructed from the fragments. The Gobelin tapestries which were designed from the start to be framed as part of the decoration are safe. The room ought to be restored.

St George's Hall is a different story. In terms of restoration, it presents no insuperable problems. The first impact of the photographs of it taken immediately after the fire is a horrifying one (Pl. 160), but if one looks at them carefully one can see that, with the exception of the narrow south wall, its walls and most of their plasterwork decoration survive virtually complete. The ceiling, also of plaster, is down; but unlike the elaborate ceiling of the Grand Reception Room it followed a relatively simple design, which could be reproduced with fidelity by taking casts.

On the other hand, it was never a very satisfactory room; it scarcely lived up to its symbolic importance as the meeting and feasting-place of one of the greatest and oldest of the orders of chivalry. The two seventeenth-century rooms which it replaced were far more interesting, as must have been the medieval hall which preceded them. Wyatville himself did not want to run the two rooms together; "this extension was not in accordance with the original design of Sir Jeffry," wrote his pupil Henry Ashton, and added, "the good effect on the whole of the addition made to its length may be doubted" The proportions that resulted were awkward; the new room became too much of a tunnel even if, through sheer size, an impressive tunnel. Neither its design nor its detailing were more than commonplace. W. St John Hope, the most learned of the Castle's historians, refers to it as "this preposterous apartment". Sir Nikolaus Pevsner, in the Berkshire volume of his *Buildings of England*, remarked that "no-one could call it very festive". It may be time for a fourth hall.

Whatever happens, something is going to change. It is only reasonable, for instance, that the major rooms which have been damaged by the fire should be opened to the public after they have been restored, in whatever form. Public money is going to restore them; and making them accessible would only be part of the historic process of private rooms becoming public, which has being going on at Windsor for eight hundred years.

If one accepts that St George's Hall, the Private Chapel, the Private Dining-room and the Octagon Room should be restored to a new design, there are obvious potentialities for re-thinking the plan of this part of the Castle, in terms of the uses to which it could be put and the kind of events that could take place there. The idea of turning St George's Hall back into two rooms has its attractions; on the other hand there are occasions when a room the size of the existing one can be useful, and the solution might be two rooms that could be opened up into one on special occasions, or vice versa.

The prospect of architects, painters, sculptors and other artists and craftsmen collaborating to produce a new St George's Hall is an exciting one. It is a room with a great tradition behind it; there is nothing wrong with tradition, but it needs to be re-stated to make it relevant, as has happened in St George's Hall in the past, and could happen again. A new Hall will only be worthwhile if those working on it can be inspired by the commission; otherwise the result will be lifeless or pretentious, and it would have been better to restore what was there before. Perhaps St George and the Dragon could be a starting point; as symbols of good fighting against evil they are as relevant today as they have ever been.

The fire has happened at a critical moment when the role, image and future of the monarchy are the subject of debate. The restoration could show that that monarchy is still relevant today, and that it stands for values that are important. It is a challenge and an opportunity for both Queen and Government.

Early in March 1993, I wrote to a number of architects and artists, including lighting and stage designers. I invited them to submit ideas for what might be done to St George's Hall, for inclusion in my book and also for exhibition in the Architecture Foundation's gallery in Bury Street, London. I suggested that, if they felt like it, they might collaborate with others of their choice, not necessarily drawn from my original list. Those who accepted were supplied with plans, sections, elevations and photographs, and with views of the Hall at its various stages, but were left free to suggest whatever they wanted, in any form they liked. Some provided drawings and text, some drawings only.

I tried to choose a mixture of people of different ages, and with different approaches. Although I took advice from the Architecture Foundation, the choice remained a personal one; there were, for example, no modern classicists on the original list, as although I am convinced that the language of classical architecture is as usable today as it ever was, I know of no contemporary English architect who can re-interpret it to my satisfaction.

I could offer very little time, and for this or other reasons a number of those I asked felt that they had to refuse. In all fourteen people submitted ideas, individually or in partnership, and it is these which are reproduced in the following pages. I am extremely grateful to everyone who contributed, for so freely giving their time and trouble to the project.

I have been impressed by the quality of what has come in, and the different approaches which lie behind it. Various themes can be picked out, by no means exclusive of each other. One is the creation of beautiful or exciting roofs, sometimes inspired by historic precedents, but using contemporary technology and materials. One is the introduction of light, in all kinds of ways, to change the room from a static to a dynamic one. Another approach derives from the realisation that St George's Hall is a stage set for dramatic events, and the devising of new ways of setting these off. Designs have been used to convey all kinds of symbolic or historic messages, whether rejecting the past and celebrating the contemporary world, or using heraldry or the historic symbolism of the fight of Good against Evil in a new way. By subtle adjustments space has been re-ordered and expanded, to open up Wyatville's claustrophobic tunnel; or the Hall has been given new uses, such as the display of great works of art in the Royal Collection. Wit, strong feeling and contemporary technology have fused together.

These are not fully-worked-out schemes, but ideas produced by creative people under pressure. They make clear how much talent is available, and how sad and sterile an alternative a complete restoration would be. But I leave the designs to speak for themselves.

AN EYE FOR WINDSOR CASTLE

SIR DENYS LASDUN

Sir Denys Lasdun, architect.
Born 1914, knighted 1976,
RIBA Gold Medal, 1977. The
doyen of English architects,
his works include the Royal
College of Physicians, halls
of residence at the University
of East Anglia, the National
Theatre, and the EEC
Headquarters for the
European Investment Bank,
Luxembourg.

SIR EDUARDO PAOLOZZI

Sir Eduardo Luigi Paolozzi
RA, sculptor. Born in
Scotland of Italian parents,
1924. His works include the
murals in Tottenham Court
Road underground station.
Sculptured self-portrait in
National Portrait Gallery.

These proposals are a reinterpretation, in today's terms, of the Castle's historic ceremonial functions. The use of glass, and the introduction of a Belvedere transform St. George's Hall into a transparent space suggesting the more open monarchy that is to be.

A secondary North/South Axis has been created on the centre-line between the South/East doorway of Waterloo Chamber and the South doorway of the Grand Reception Room.

The intersection of this Axis with the roof is marked by a raised Lantern descending, free of the South wall, to form the Belvedere.

The three central fire-scarred window openings are retained as a memorial. Cills and upstands are removed allowing this section of the South wall to become an open screen giving free access to the Belvedere. All remaining walls could be restored, incorporating the arms of the Knights of the Garter. The original furniture is returned.

The glazed roof embodies photo-electric cells to generate energy and Eduardo Paolozzi takes this as his inspiration to power his mobile feature terminating the North/South Axis in the Quadrangle. It is aligned with the statue of Charles II.

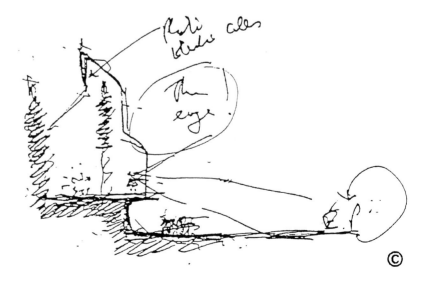

©

Inside the Belvedere

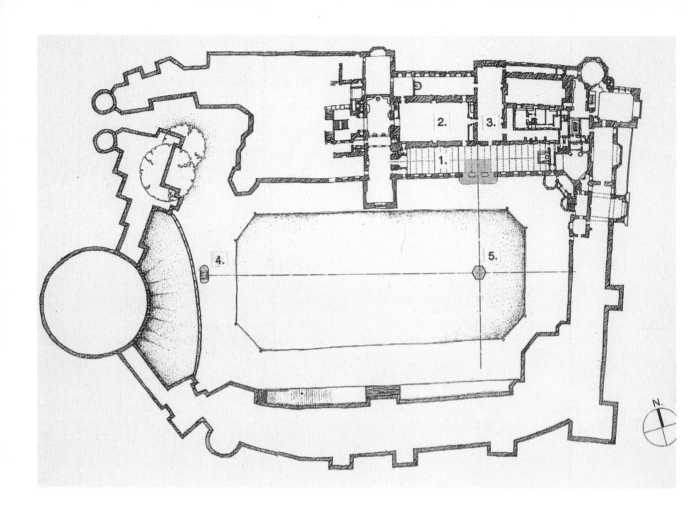

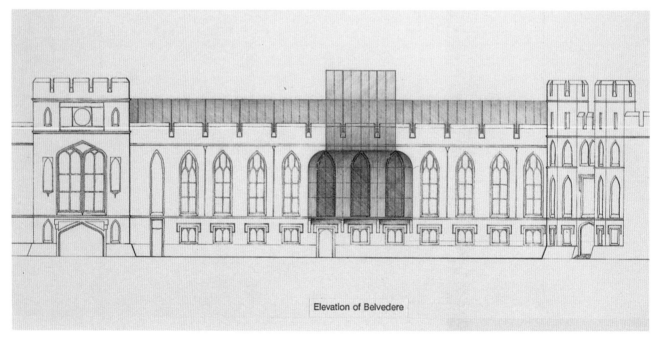

Elevation of Belvedere

IV

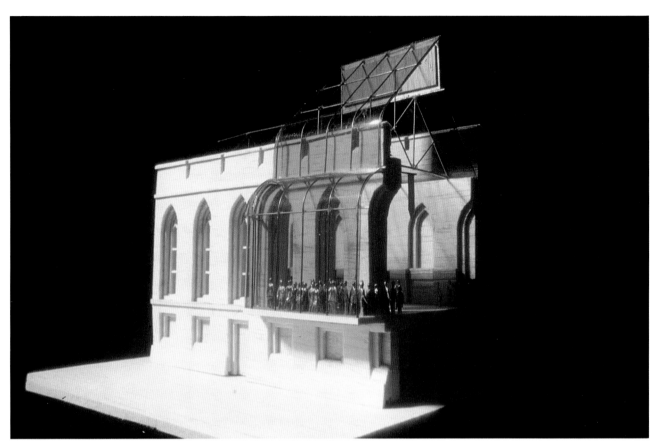

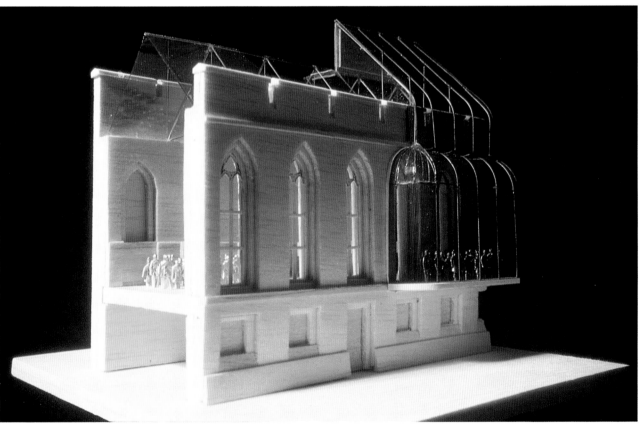

Two outside views of the Belvedere

The Roof

An elegant truss roof and lantern with mechanically connected stainless steel members supports the glazing allowing controlled daylight into the hall.

To maximise energy conservation and natural ventilation the technical proposals include solar control glass, double glazing and the use of low emissivity coatings in conjunction with computer controlled mechanically operated external blinds.

It is also proposed translucent fabric awnings will provide visual comfort at night together with carefully balanced indirect artificial illumination.

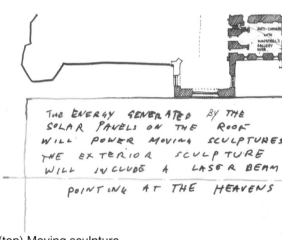

THE ENERGY GENERATED BY THE SOLAR PANELS ON THE ROOF WILL POWER MOVING SCULPTURES THE EXTERIOR SCULPTURE WILL INCLUDE A LASER BEAM POINTING AT THE HEAVENS

(top) Moving sculpture
(above) Detail of plan
(right) Eduardo Paolozzi's proposal for St George's Hall

VI

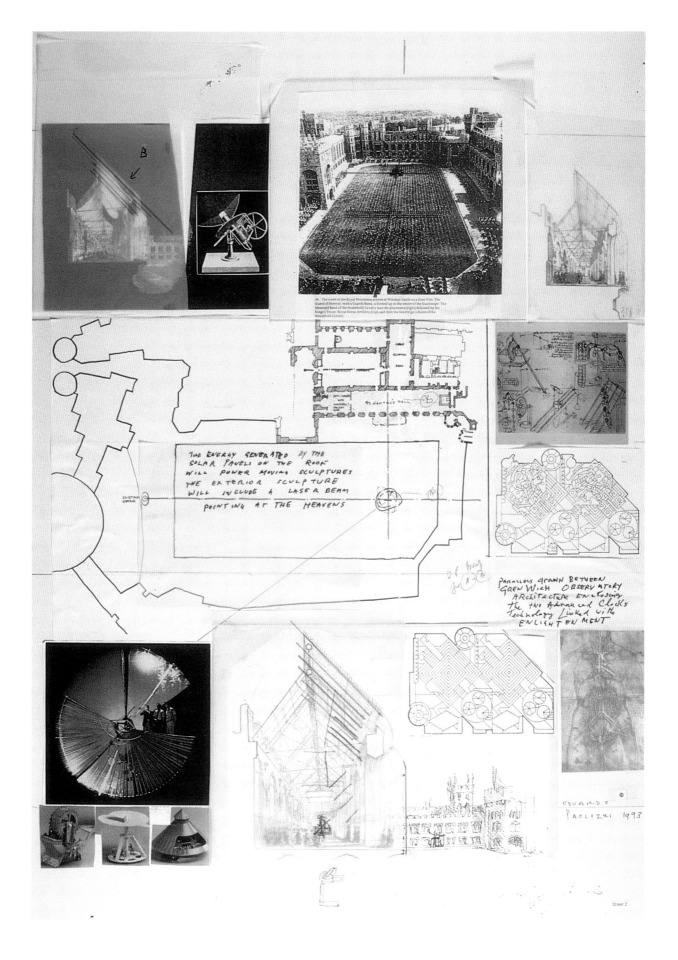

THE ENERGY GENERATED BY THE
SOLAR PANELS ON THE ROOF
WILL POWER MOVING SCULPTURES
THE EXTERIOR SCULPTURE
WILL INCLUDE A LASER BEAM
POINTING AT THE HEAVENS

PARALLELS DRAWN BETWEEN
GRENWICH OBSERVATORY
ARCHITECTURE ENCLOSING
the two Advanced Clocks
Technology Linked with
ENLIGHTENMENT

EDVARDO
PAOLOZZI 1993

Sheet 2

ALAN FLETCHER

His international design reputation is reflected by his commissions from major corporations and cultural institutions around the world. He began his career in New York where he worked for *Fortune* magazine, the Container Corporation and IBM. Moving back to London in 1962 he co-founded Fletcher/Forbes/Gill, which served such clients as Pirelli, Cunard, Penguin Books and Olivetti. Whilst working at Pentagram, which he co-founded in 1972, he created design programmes for Reuters, the Mandarin Oriental Hotel Group, the Victoria and Albert Museum, Lloyd's of London, Daimler Benz, Arthur Andersen and Co, and ABB. He left Pentagram to open his own studio in 1992. He has received gold awards from the British Designers and Art Directors Association and the New

St Georges Hall, Windsor Castle. The debate revolves around whether to reconstruct or redesign the space. My inclination is to do neither, but leave the gutted and charred remains exactly as they are. —

My proposal is to throw a glass canopy over the exposed roof, insert a freestanding, narrow steel deck on stilts down the centre of the aisle, with an elegant light staircase of steel and glass.

Hanging from the roof, and slung below the deck, are projectors (film/video/slide) to throw images onto different areas of the ruined interior. These would recreate the various decorative styles the hall has undergone in the past: Gothic, Baroque, Victorian — the conflagration itself — and of course the new proposals.

The consantly changing images would create a theatrical backdrop for the functions taking place on the deck: ceremonies, Garter lunches, state banquets, Royal investitures, masked balls etc.

Note: In 1999 a supper was held by the Architecture Foundation, in the hall, to finally resolve the continuing debate of whether to restore or redesign. To pass the time I did a sketch on my serviette of the interior — an impression of the projected imagery, as seen looking down the aisle from my seat on the deck. Alan Fletcher. 1/4/93

York "One Show". In 1977 he shared the Designers and Art Directors Association President's Award for outstanding contributions to design with Pentagram partner Colin Forbes. In 1982 the Society of Industrial Artists and Designers awarded him the Annual Medal for outstanding achievement in design. He served as President of the Designers and Art Directors Association in 1973, and as President of the Alliance Graphique Internationale from 1982 to 1985. He is a Royal Designer for Industry, a Fellow of the Chartered Society of Designers and a Senior Fellow of the Royal College of Art.

Books he has co-authored include *Identity Kits - a pictorial survey of visual signs*; *Graphic Design - a visual comparison*; *A Sign System Manual* and four publications on the work of Pentagram: *Pentagram - the work of five designers*, *Living by Design*, *Ideas of Design* and *The Compendium*.

Alan Fletcher trained at the Royal College of Art in London and the School of Architecture and Design at Yale University.

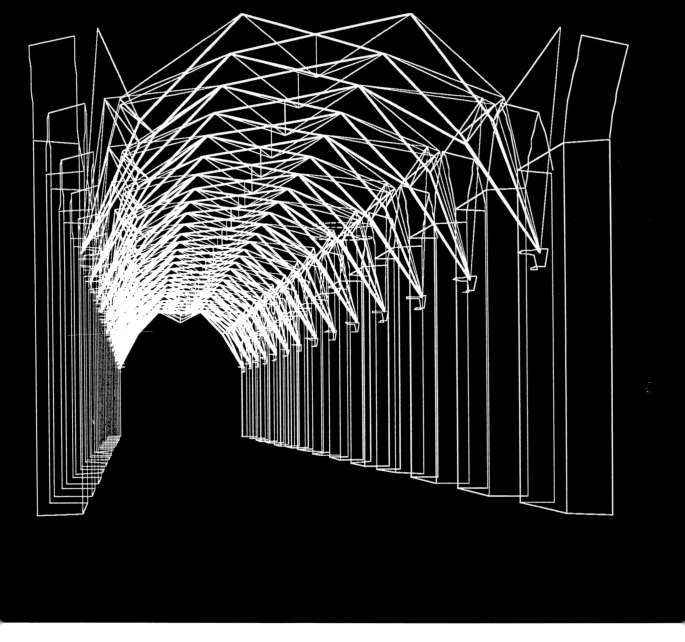

RICHARD CORNELIUS MacCORMAC

Born 3 September 1938. Graduated with First Class Honours, University of Cambridge, 1962. Travelled in the United States, and worked for Powell & Moya in 1963, before going into private practice in 1969. Richard MacCormac is a Fellow of the Royal Society of Arts, a member of the Royal Fine Art Commission, and served as chairman of the RIBA Awards 1990 (Wessex Region Jury). He was President of the Royal Institute of British Architects from 1991-93.

"The restoration of St George's Hall could be seen to pose a nineteenth century stylistic dilemma. There can be no obviously authentic restoration because of the transformation of the interior from a medieval timber

X

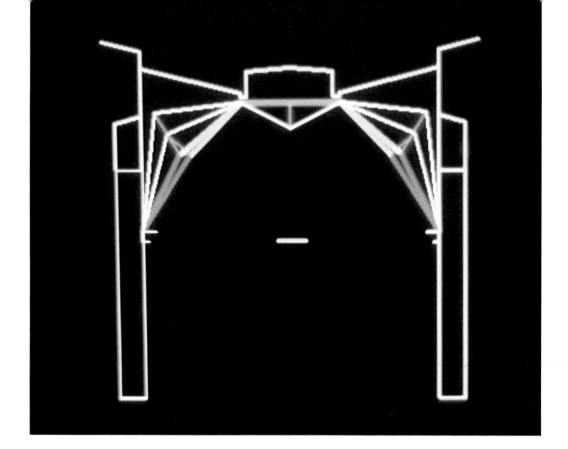

Views of roof

structure to a classical banqueting hall and then to the decorative gothic of Wyatville.

Our proposal is closer to the medieval structure than to the other interpretations of the interior. It has been derived from the principles of ribbed gothic vaulting and is constructed of hardwood shafts in compression, connected by polished bronze alloy bosses, the whole assembly stabilised by tracery of polished bronze alloy in tension.

As in a gothic building the shafts will tend to obscure the clerestory windows when seen obliquely, so that the impression of luminosity will be conveyed by the structure itself rather than by the window apertures. The timber structure is polychromatic and the whole enlivened by the sparkle of the polished bronze alloy bosses and tracery, lit by the windows and by small apertures in the roof which would admit occasional shafts of sunlight."

Roof views

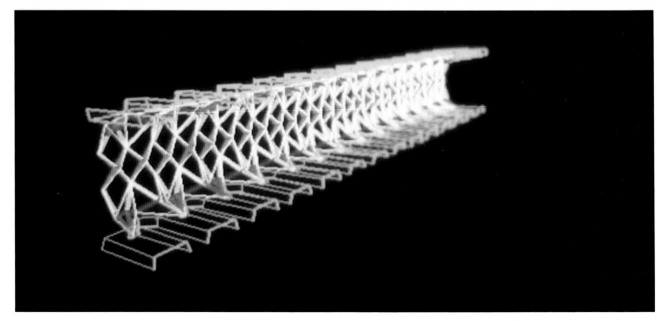

DAVID CHIPPERFIELD &
MICHAEL CRAIG MARTIN

David Chipperfield trained at the Architectural Association and worked for Douglas Stephen, Richard Rogers and Foster Associates. David Chipperfield Architects was established in 1984 and has carried out work in England, France, USA and Japan, where the practice opened a Tokyo office in 1987. Current projects include the National Rowing Museum at Henley-on-Thames.

Michael Craig Martin, artist, was born in Dublin, grew up in the States, and has lived in Great Britain since 1966. He had a Retrospective at the Whitechapel Art Gallery in 1989, and has shown throughout the world. He is a trustee of the Tate Gallery.

"David chipperfield and I have collaborated on this proposal. We decided that the scale and nature of the problem called for an overall architectural solution, not one involving separate aspects of art and architecture. We felt that we could either make a radi
Michael Craig Martin, artist, was born Michael Craig Martin, artist, was born in Dublin, grew up in the States, and has lived in Great Britain since 1966. He had a retrospective at the Whitechapel Art Gallery in 1989, and has shown

throughout the world. He is a trustee of the Tate Gallery.

"David Chipperfield and I have collaborated on this proposal. We decided that the scale and nature of the problem called for an overall architectural solution, not one involving separate aspects of art and architecture. We felt that we could either make a radical and unrealizable proposal or, given the inherent theatricality of the space and its function, make a proposal both understated and plausible. We decided on the latter.

From the photographs both before and after the fire, it was obvious that the ceiling was the most distressing physical loss, but the least distressing aesthetically: heavy, over decorated, artificial in every way, absurdly expensive to recreate. Pictures of earlier states of the hall show very different

ceilings, each of which dominates the character of the hall. Our proposal focuses on the creation of a new ceiling.

We came to the conclusion that the lower level of the hall, the level at which people move and dine, the level of the decorative oak panelling incorporating the gothic windows and arches should be restored to more or less its previous state. While the 'antique' aspect of the hall may itself be historically bogus, it uses a language of materials and images that speak of grandeur, majesty, and history for which we (fortunately) have no contemporary equivalent. A new ceiling would acknowledge the links with the past while redefining the hall in modern terms. For the new ceiling, we propose using a traditional material, wood, principally oak (with its reference to the original mediaeval roof),

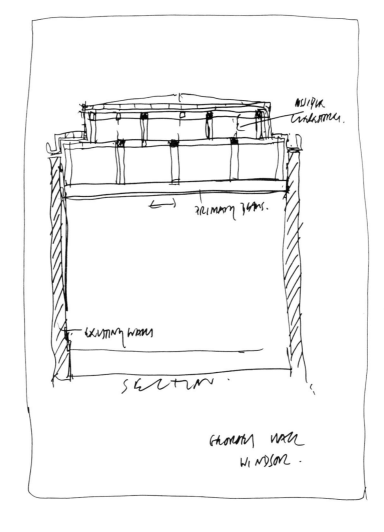

Original drawng for ceiling by Chipperfield and Craig-Martin.

MARK FISHER & STUART HOPPS,
Casaverde Construction Inc.

Mark Fisher trained at the
Architectural Association. Partner
in Fisher Park, he has designed
rock 'n' roll shows including Pink
Floyd's "The Wall", the Rolling
Stones' "Steel Wheels", and U2's
"Zoo TV".

Stuart Hopps graduated in
Engineering from UCLA. He is a
partner with Chip Faulks in
Casaverde Construction Inc.
Stuart Hopps projects include the
Landslip House, Sunland, CA, and
the Big Shed, China Lake, CA.

He drives a silver 1973 Cadillac
Coupe de Ville.

Proposals for St George's Hall

CORRUPTION
Conservation by the State recruits the past into the processes of the present. It attempts to preserve a history that has been erased by the loss of Empire, immigration, and the Information Age. As the consequences of these changes threaten traditional power structures, the State responds by encouraging the Heritage Industry to create a mythic common history in which the aristocracy and their subjects share a pastoral Arcadia.

APOCALYPSE
The fire of November 1992 has stripped away Wyatville's artificial architecture and left the authentic Plantagenet hall and chapel as a ruin. The conflagration has destroyed five hundred years of self-aggrandising myth creation, and restored the real architecture of the past. The flames have revealed the true architecture and landscape of the twentieth century in the skies above the castle.

REDEMPTION
Our proposal breaks through the synthetic nature of Heritage to reveal the genuine contemporary landscape. We preserve the aristocratic ruin whilst exploring the free movements of peoples in the flight paths overhead. The burnt-out shell is re-gilded by light that responds to the changing elements. The space is extended beyond earth to the galaxies, providing an experience that transcends the fragility of man's vanity, greed and power.

SPECIFICATION
1.0 Existing structure
All masonry walls to be stabilised.

Floor to be re-laid where necessary, using original boards, and swept. Window glass to be left as is.

2.0 New structure
Galvanised tubular steel scaffolding erected to form structural enclosure spanning between the Quadrangle and the north wall of St George's Hall, leaving 1m wide opening running the entire length of the Hall, precisely aligned with Heathrow runway 09/27.

3.0 Cladding
PVC-coated polyester sheeting laminated both sides with vacuum-deposited gold-coated mylar film, made up with grommets at 300 c/c and laced to structure. Cladding to edges of opening to be finished on site.

4.0 Lighting
100no. high-pressure sodium motorway lights placed inside the gap between the ruin and the enclosure, illuminating the golden tarpaulins.

5.0 Furniture
All original furniture to be kept in store. Dining furniture to be withdrawn from store as required.

6.0 Public access
There shall be public access at all times.

Mark Fisher, with Stuart Hopps of Casaverde Construction Inc.
13 April, 1993.

TOM McPHILLIPS

Tom McPhillips is a Production Designer based in London and on the United States East Coast. Major credits include the design of tours for Michael Jackson, Diana Ross and The Who. He has worked for a wide range of acts in the business including Heavy Metal, Pop, and Country music. He has also designed sets for television, exhibitions, TV commercials and musicals.

Currently he designs the "Unplugged" series for MTV.

He studied sculpture at St Martin's School of Art in London, then began working as a design assistant for the Young Vic. Deciding to specialise as a Scenic Artist, he worked for the John Campbell Studio for three years. He then went to the English National Opera, where he worked as a Propmaker. In 1977 he set up his own studio.

WINDSOR CASTLE

ROOF BECOMES SKYLIGHT WINEGLASS COLUMNS HAVE LIGHT FROM ABOVE DURING DAY, LIT FROM BELOW AT NIGHT. WALLS ARE MIRRORED AT GROUND LEVEL CRYSTAL TUBES HANG FROM SKYLIGHT. WINEGLASS COLUMNS SUGGEST THE CELEBRATORY ASPECT OF THE BUILDING.

Tom McPhillips '93

In the early 1980s he designed and supplied sets for numerous pop videos, including "Ebony and Ivory" for Paul McCartney and Stevie Wonder, and a television special for Ashford and Simpson. From 1982 onwards, he began to design for Rock Concerts. His first designs were for Gary Numan, Nik Kershaw, and a series of shows for Culture Club. His early American tours were for a variety of Heavy Metal bands, including Ozzy Osbourne, Judas Priest, and Dio. Concert Tour stage designs have included: Michael Jackson, Judas Priest, Diana Ross, The Who, Twisted Dister, Emerson Lake and Palmer, GTR (Steves Howe and Hackett), Scorpions, Luther Vandross, Twisted Sister, Robert Plant, Elo-2, Def Leppard and Barry Manilow.

He has submitted four different ideas for St George's Hall.

TOTAL
SKYLIGHT ABOVE.

PAINTED/STAINED
GLASS
HANGING △'S

GLASS TUBE
WALLS

THE 'GLASS' ROOM.

Tom McPhillips '93

XX

WINDSOR CASTLE · GOTHIC GLASS.   TOM MCPHILLIPS '93

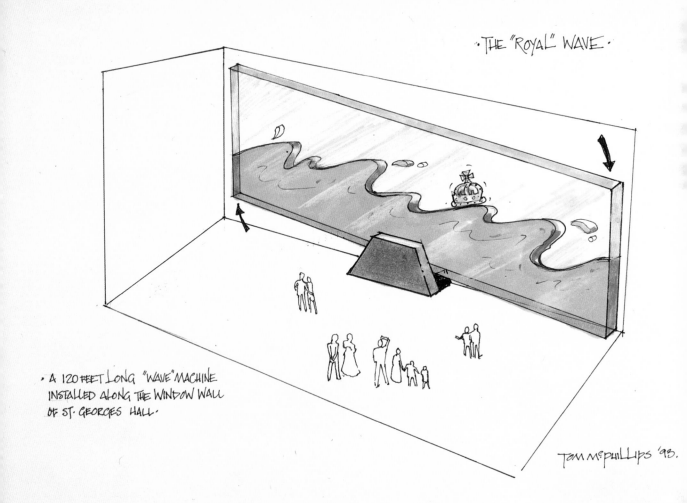

· THE "ROYAL" WAVE ·

· A 120 FEET LONG "WAVE" MACHINE
INSTALLED ALONG THE WINDOW WALL
OF ST· GEORGES HALL·

Tom McPhillips '93·

MICHAEL HOPKINS CBE RA

Awarded CBE for services to architecture in 1989. Royal Academician, 1992. Commissioner, Royal Fine Art Commission, 1986 - present. Member of the London Advisory Committee of English Heritage, 1990-93. Member of RIBA Council, 1991- present. Vice-President of the Architectural Association 1987-89 and 1991-93. Trustee, Thomas Cubitt Trust. Past and current Assessor for the RIBA, *Financial Times*, and Civic Trust Award Schemes. Founder Partner, Michael Hopkins & Partners, 1976- present. Partner, Foster Associates, 1969-75. Tom Hancock Architects and Partners, 1965-66. Leonard Manasseh and Partners, 1963-65. Student, Architectural Association, 1959-62.

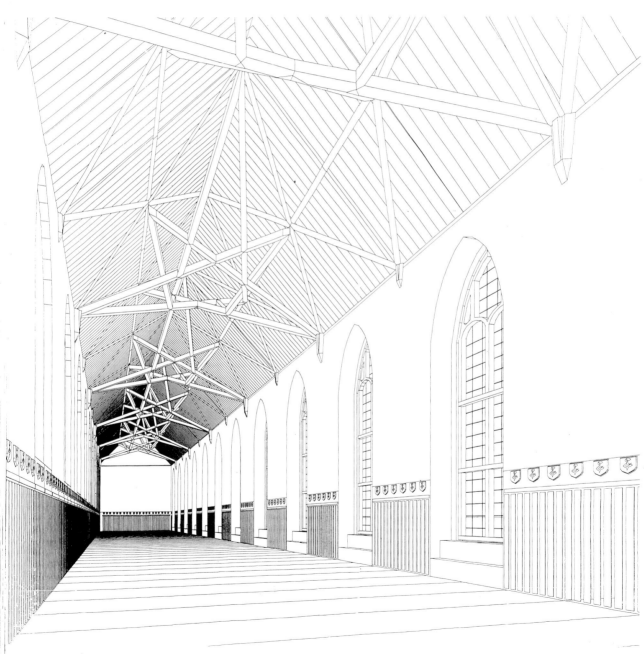

Star of the Garter

Looking directly at roof from beneath.

A Proposal for the Reconstruction of St George's Hall at Windsor Castle

The appalling fire at Windsor Castle does provide the opportunity to consider again the original form and volume of Edward III's great Hall and to think again about its association with the Order of the Garter.

Both the reconstruction for Charles II and that for George IV, although splendid in their own terms and time, employed lower ceilings, doing away with the open roof and expressive timber roof structure of the fourteenth century Hall.

Could we not now return to the original spatial volume and develop a contemporary solution closer in spirit to Edward III's Hall where the decoration grows out of an elaboration of the structural framework?

Using the original walls and window openings and inspired by the form of the Garter Star, we are proposing a new finely engineered timber roof structure, based on a stellar form, which will be both functional and reminiscent of the Hall's long association with the Order of the Garter.

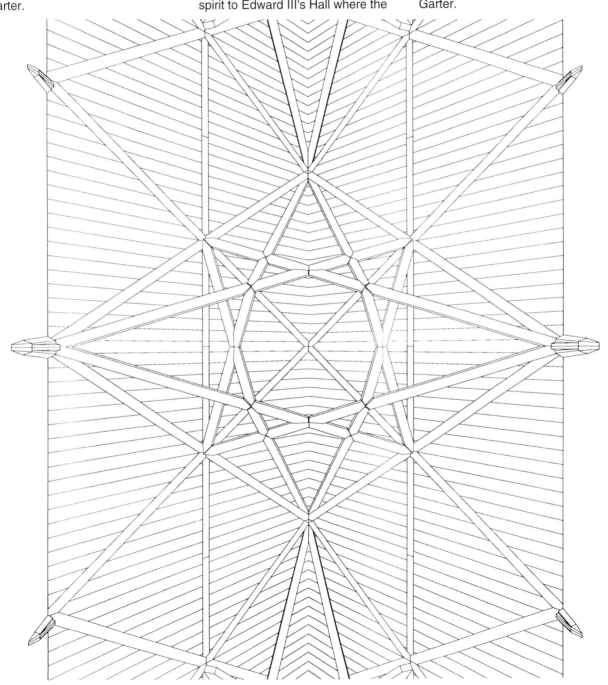

TOM PHILLIPS, with NICOLA
HICKS

"Why *Curriculum Vitae*? Are those
not the world's dullest documents, a
yawn to produce or peruse?"

Tom Phillips. *Works and Text*
(1992), p. 25.

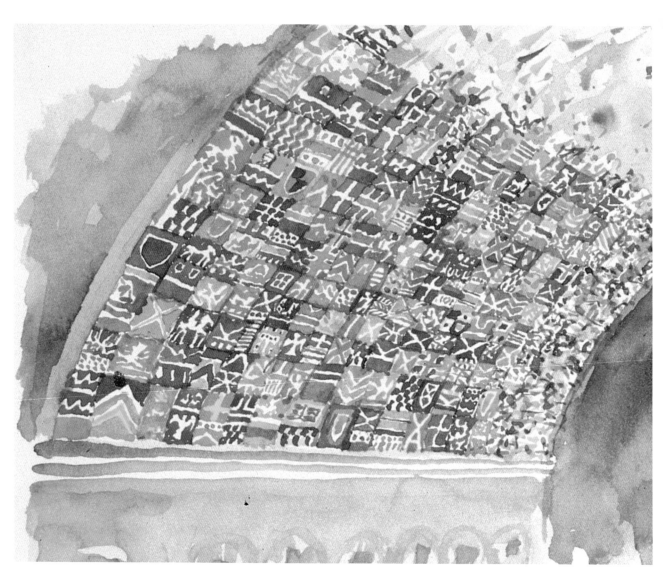

CEILING

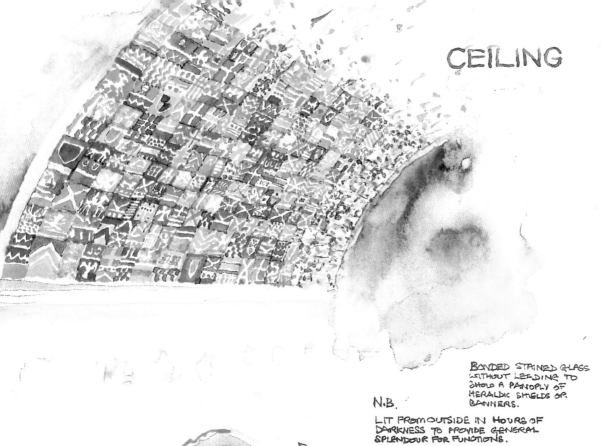

For the Great Hall at Windsor. TOM PHILLIPS R.A.

BONDED STAINED GLASS
WITHOUT LEADING TO
SHOW A PANOPLY OF
HERALDIC SHIELDS OR
BANNERS.

N.B.

LIT FROM OUTSIDE IN HOURS OF
DARKNESS TO PROVIDE GENERAL
SPLENDOUR FOR FUNCTIONS.

Walls otherwise plain except for roundels of bronze
heads of notable figures from science & arts etc. in
British history.

Tapestry to take up theme of
Light challenging darkness
via episodes from British
Life. ie Freeing of Slaves,
Emancipation of women etc.
Civil rather than military
victories over evil.......

WALLS

Tapestry in
sections but
a continuous
fabric.

AT FAR END AGAINST
TAPESTRY WITH RICH
BUT SUBDUED COLOURS
A POLYCHROME STATUE
BY NICOLA HICKS OF
ST GEORGE & THE DRAGON

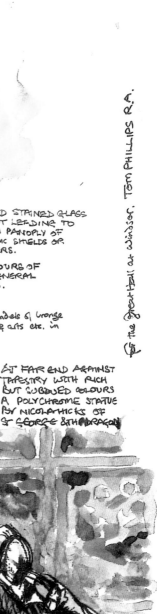

Sketches of sculpture
by Nicola Hicks.

Drawing of sculpture by Nicola Hicks

British history.

Tapestry in
Sections but
a continuous
fabric.

AT FAR END AGAINST
TAPESTRY WITH RICH
BUT SUBDUED COLOURS
A POLYCHROME STATUE
BY NICOLA HICKS OF
ST GEORGE & THE DRAGON

Sketches of sculpture
by Nicola Hicks.

XXVIII

ERIC PARRY

Eric Parry studied at the University of Newcastle-upon-Tyne, the Royal College of Art, the Architectural Association and Cambridge University. In independent practice, he has designed an office building at Stukeley Park, and the interiors for the head office of Stanhope Properties, and the house of Stuart Lipton. He has recently designed a studio for the artist Tom Phillips.

The Hall would incorporate Mantegna's "Triumph of Caesar" cartoons, now at Hampton Court. The stuccoed ceiling would be painted with celestial and arboreal motifs. Heraldic tapestries on the window wall would act as an acoustic damper and light baffle. The iconography of St George and the Garter would be the basis of a sculptural programme in the separate Chapel.

E.P. 9.93

RON HERRON

Born London. Founder member of Archigram. Director of Urban Design with William L. Pereira and Associates, Los Angeles (1969-70). Partner Archigram Architects (1970-75), Partner Pentagram Design (1977-81), formed Ron Herron Associates in 1982, joined by son Andrew in 1985, formed Heron Associates in 1985, formed Herron Associates © Imagination in 1989. Herron Associates is now an inde-pendent company again (1993). Recent projects include the re-mod-elling of 25 Store Street, South Crescent for Imagination, Canada Water underground station on the new Jubilee line extension, and three projects in Toyama, Japan. Currently working on Urban Design and other projects in Japan. Teaches at the Architectural Association (since 1966) and at the Bartlett School of Architecture where he holds a Chair and is a Visiting Professor.

SETS FIT FOR/ THE QUEEN -
WINDSOR/ VERSION.

Make reference to the early (1975)
project 'sets fit for The Queen'.
The Queen as superstar........
The Palace (castle) as 'movie' stage....
St Georges Hall as 'SET'!........
'ceremonial SET'

SET as in theatre set/movie
set/setting/scenery/masque/
set piece/.

implication....
The environment in change/
Temporary/paper thin/
Responsive/changeable/
indeterminate/choice.
To suit mood/event/audience/
fantasy/whim/act/ceremony/
public/private/dream......
The expected image or
conversely the unexpected -
to suit the situation.
The Queen as superstar.

windsor castle.   MA. 20.4.93.

XXXI

SETS CONTINUED...........DINING

RON HERRON JUNE 1976

A NOTE ON THE SOURCES

The standard works on the architecture of Windsor Castle, including the Lower Ward and St George's Chapel, are W. St John Hope's monumental *Windsor Castle: an Architectural History* (2 vols, 1914), and the Windsor sections in *History of the Royal Works* (ed Howard Colvin, 1963-82) (vols 2, 3, 5 and 6). There is a shorter article by W. St John Hope in Volume III of the Victoria County History, *Berkshire*, which also contains a useful account of the history of the Castle and Parks. Basic sources of illustrations, together with short descriptive text, are W.A. Pyne *Royal Residences* (1819), Henry Ashton (ed) *Illustrations of Windsor Castle by the late Sir Jeffry Wyatville* (1841), and Joseph Nash *Windsor Castle* (1848). The drawings and watercolours of Windsor by the Sandby brothers are catalogued in A.J. Oppé *Sandby Drawings at Windsor Castle* (1947), and a selection illustrated in Jane Roberts (ed) *A Souvenir Album of Sandby Views of Windsor* (1990).

Among historical accounts and topographical descriptions Joseph Pote *History and Antiquities of Windsor Castle* (1749, with numerous later editions), the account of the Castle in the Berkshire section of Joseph Lysons *Magna Britannia*, vol I, and R.R. Tighe and J.E. Davis *Annals of Windsor* (2 vols, 1858), are still essential sources. Numerous shorter accounts of Windsor Castle have been published, including Sir Owen Morshead *Windsor Castle* (1951), A.E. Rowse *Windsor Castle in the History of the Nation* (1974), Christopher Hibbert *The Court at Windsor* (1964), and Robin Mackworth Young *The History and Treasures of Windsor Castle* (Pitkin Guide, n.d.), the last still in print.

Chapter 2   The Return to Camelot

Elias Ashmole *The Institution, Laws and Ceremonies of the Most Noble Order of the Garter* (1672) remains the standard history of the Order. See also J. Anstis *Register of the Order of the Garter* (1724), and Sir N.H. Nicholas *History of Orders of Knighthood* (1841-2). Other sources used for this chapter include J. Vale *Edward III and Chivalry* (Woodbridge, 1988), E.A. Jones *The Plate of St George's Chapel, Windsor Castle* (1939), and Derek Lindstrum *Sir Jeffry Wyatville, Architect to the King* (Oxford, 1972). For Victoria and Albert's sympathy with chivalry see my *Return to Camelot: Chivalry and the English Gentleman* (New Haven and London, 1981).

Chapter 3   Housing the Monarch

The main source for royal Household regulations, including those of Charles II, is Society of Antiquaries *Collection of Ordinances and Regulations for the Government of the Royal Household* (1790). Further regulations for Charles II's household exist in manuscript in Nottingham University, Portland MSS PWV92. The account of the Bantam visit is in *London Gazette*, 16 May, 1682, quoted by Tighe and Davis. The 1688 inventory (p. 56) is in the British Library Harleian MS 1890, f.25.

For George III at Windsor see John Brooke *George III* (1972), Olwen Headley *Queen Charlotte* (1975), and Charles Knight *Passage of a Working Life* (1864) vol I.

There are many biographies of George IV, but I have used especially Christopher Hibbert *George IV* (1973), and Robert Huish *Memoire of George IV* (1831). Many of Morel and Seddon's designs are illustrated in Sotheby's catalogue *Designs for the Private Apartments at Windsor Castle* for the sale on 9 April, 1970. Charles C.F. Greville *Journal*, covering the period 1818-52 (ed Henry Reeve, 1875-82) has interesting Windsor entries for the reigns of George IV, William IV and Victoria.

There are numerous memoirs etc. of members of Queen Victoria's Household. I have used especially Mrs. Hugh Wyndham (ed) *Correspondence of Sarah Spencer, Lady Lyttelton, 1787-1870* (1912); Eleanor Stanley *Twenty Years at Court* (1916); John Bailey (ed) *The Diary of Lady Frederick Cavendish* (1927); *Recollections of Louisa, Countess of Antrim (née Louisa Jane Grey)* (Shipston-on-Stour, 1937); Victor Mallet (ed) *Life with Queen Victoria: Marie Mallet's letters from Court, 1887-1901* (1968); Mary Lutyens (ed) *Lady Lytton's Court Diary, 1895-1899* (1961); and Frederick Ponsonby *Recollections of Three Reigns* (1951; his is the story about Baron de Constant on p. 80). Transcripts of Queen Victoria's diary are in the Royal Archive. Her account of the Windsor visit of Napoleon III is published in *Leaves from a Journal*, with introduction by Raymond Mortimer (1961), and there are further extracts in *Life at the Court of Queen Victoria*, ed B. St J. Nevill (Exeter, 1984).

The quotation on p. 79 and much of the information on p. 80 come from *The Private Life of the Queen* by "One of Her Majesty's Servants" (published 1897, reprinted, with introduction by Emily Sheffield, 1979). The original edition is said to have caused offense and been "withdrawn by Royal Command", but it is in fact a by no means unfriendly and apparently accurate account of the way Windsor was lived in by the Queen in the 1890s.

The recollections of A.G. Seymour, referred to on p. 84, run up to the reign of George V, and exist in a manuscript now in the Royal Archives; the information on the re-decoration of the Blue Room (p. 72) comes from this.

Chapter 4   Royal Servants

There is no proper study of this aspect of English royal life, at Windsor or anywhere else. For earlier centuries I have used the Household Regulations noted under Chapter 3 and A.R. Myers *The Household of Edward IV* (Manchester, 1959). For Chiffinch see David Allen "The Political Function of Charles II's Chiffinch" *Huntington Library Quarterly* (San Marino, California, May 1976) and Mrs Masham's letter (p. 97) is printed in *Letters to and from Henrietta, Countess of Suffolk* (1824) vol I, pp. 292-3. For the Household under Queen Victoria I have used W.J. Thoms *The Book of the Court* (1838), W.A. Lindsay *The Royal Household* (1898), the rare and anonymous *Sketches of Her Majesty's Household* (1848; copy in Royal Archives; none in British Library; in spite of its title this contains a detailed account of the different departments), and other Royal Archives material, including menu lists, the wage list of the Inspector's staff at Windsor, and A.G. Seymour's memoirs; the table in Pl 112 mainly derives from this material and the census returns for 1871 and 1881 (copies in Windsor Public Library). There is no proper study of Prince Albert's reforms, but something about them in Vera Watson *A Queen at Home* (1952), based on the Lord Chamberlain's papers in the Public Record Office. The description of the kitchen on p. 107 is from *The Private Life of Queen Victoria*. For Gabriel Tschumi's and F.J. Corbett's memoirs, see *Royal Chef* (1954), and *Fit for a King* (1956). There is much useful information in *Royal Encyclopaedia* (ed Ronald Allison and Sarah Riddell, 1991), including a table of the modern Master of the Household's department on p. 337.

Chapter 5   The Village on the Hill

In addition to Hope, I have used the publications in the "Historical Monographs relating to St George's Chapel, Windsor Castle" series, especially S.L. Ollard *The Deans and Canons of St George's Chapel* (1950), E.H. Fellowes *The Minor Canons of St George's Chapel* (1945), and the same author's *The Military Knights of Windsor, 1352-1944* (1944), all published in Windsor. The childhood recollections referred to on p. 126 derive from Louisa Gray's *Recollections* (see Chapter 3), Mary MacCarthy *A Nineteenth Century Childhood* (1924) and Maurice Baring *A Puppet Show of Memory* (1922).

Chapter 6   Royal Recreations

In addition to general works already listed, sources for this chapter include William Menzies *Windsor Great Park* (in the superior 1864 edition); Marcus Binney "Sported in by Kings: Windsor Great Park" *Country Life* 30 July, 1981; Owen Morshead *George IV and Royal Lodge* (Brighton, 1965), G.E. Chambers "The 'Ruins' at Virginia Water" *Berkshire Archaeological Journal*, vol 54 (1954-5), pp. 39-52, and Robert Rhodes James *Albert Prince Consort* (1983).

ILLUSTRATION CREDITS

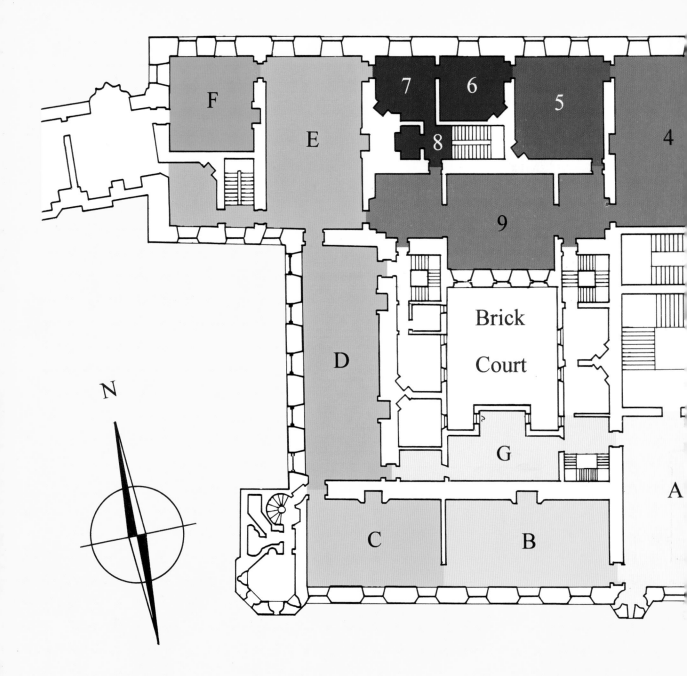

1 King's Guard Chamber

2 King's Presence Chamber

3 King's Privy Chamber

4 King's Drawing Room

5 King's Great Bedchamber

6 King's Little Bedchamber

7 King's Closet

8 King's Backstairs

9 King's Eating Room